WEAR A KILLER OUTFIT

Wear A Killer Outfit

And Other Advice for Speaking Publicly

ROBIN STOMBLER

 BWT Productions

ISBN: 979-8-9866627-0-1

Library of Congress Control Number: 2022913944

Cover design by Courtney Garvin
Printed in the United States of America

First Printing, 2022

BWT Productions
Arlington, VA

Dedicated to Marianna Fillmore
Because coaches have a lasting impact

Contents

Find Your Voice

"Third place goes to . . ." Sitting on the steps in the back of an auditorium on the University of Virginia campus, I was hopeful, but not confident, that I might score a win at the state championship for extemporaneous speaking. Third place went to a girl from another part of Virginia. My coach, Marianna Fillmore, and I stole a glance. We knew my performance was not my best, and if I didn't rank third, then I likely wouldn't medal at all.

"And in second place . . ." At this point, my name hadn't been called and I was quite sure it was over. I was a senior in high school, and forensics—a public speaking club—was one of my favorite activities, but I knew there was another competitor who was destined for the top slot. Then I heard, "First place for extemporaneous speaking goes to Robin Stombler." I shot my coach an "are they crazy?" look as my Blacksburg High School forensics teammates cheered. I stood, made my way down the stairs of the auditorium, and accepted the medal, a bit sheepishly.

I kept the criticism sheets I received from the judges on that day of competition. My randomly-drawn question asked if George Bush should be the Republican candidate for US President. I don't recall if I argued in the affirmative or the negative, but according to the judges, my thought content was "superior" and "very well organized." Evidently, I did "exceptionally well" when it came to providing concrete, supporting details, and the analogy I provided was "brilliant" and showed "good imagination and creativity." I was told I had a "tremendous amount of style and stage presence" and was invited to join the University of Virginia team for college. Forget about saving these critiques, I should have had them framed.

Extemporaneous speaking, or "extemp" as the cool kids called it, belonged to the sport of forensics. The word "forensics" translates to a forum for public discussion and debate, but in high school it meant any one of a number of speaking categories, such as: original oratory, prose reading, poetry, spelling, and, yes, extemp. In college, the number of categories expanded to include dramatic duo, impromptu, after dinner speaking, and more.

When I was a sophomore, my Spanish language teacher, Mrs. Fillmore, said she was going to coach a forensics team and asked me to join. Each of us in this very small inaugural group tested different categories to see which ones fit us best. Extemp had my name written all over it.

Extemporaneous speaking involves blindly selecting a random, current events–related question. Questions might address international or domestic affairs, politics, economics, popular culture, or scientific topics. Each participant had thirty minutes to research the given topic (without use of the internet), then deliver a five-minute analytical, sometimes persuasive, speech to a panel of judges. The critics would assess your speech for its logic and depth of thought, for its use of supporting details and comprehension, and for the sincerity, poise, and voice of its speaker.

The pressure of delivering cogent remarks on an often-unknown issue was exhilarating to me. As a kid, I devoured the news, and extemp was a way to process whatever knowledge I may have gained. I was, and arguably still am, reserved by nature, yet I usually had a compulsion to speak up when I had a strong opinion or when I felt a need to right a wrong. Extemp provided me with the skills to organize and present thoughts more clearly as well as gain confidence to speak up more readily.

This book is not intended to turn you into an extemp master or entice you into the forensics world. It is meant to share with you the importance of finding and using your voice. Many of my personal stories unfold in these pages, but it is the experiences of others that may be particularly meaningful to you. I reached out to former teammates and to high school students I coached long ago to ask them how their forensics skills impacted their lives. Their stories are captivating and encouraging. Their successes in life are a testament to the power of using their voices. You will also find many tips to help improve your public speaking skills, no matter if you are a teenager entering the world of forensics competition or an adult already immersed in your career.

Use your voice. The world is waiting to hear you.

Chapter One

Tackle the Fear

Public speaking can be terrifying. Glossophobia, or the fear of speaking in public, manifests itself in many people and in many ways. Some run frantically to a restroom before going on stage. Others are so nervous their hands shake and their voice quivers. I have been told stories of people who will quit jobs or leave school if they are required to stand up to give a speech. This fear may attack no matter your station in life.

Prince Harry, Duke of Sussex and a member of the British royal family, revealed his secret in a 2014 #FeelNoShame campaign: He gets "incredibly nervous before public speaking no matter how big the crowd or the audience."[i]

You don't have to be famous to find sweat rolling down your brow or butterflies whirling in your stomach. While providing a routine update for an association task force, I nonchalantly called on a couple of colleagues to add their perspectives on the subject matter. Both individuals eloquently added their own opinions. Yet, afterwards, I received personal notes of apology and concern. One person wrote, "Sorry I was not prepared or used to impromptu questions. I hope to improve in the future." It surprised me to learn how uncomfortable these individuals were with this informal request for public comment.

Speaking up, whether to thousands in a crowd or to a small group of colleagues, can indeed be terrifying for anyone. It is said that US President Thomas Jefferson, for all his recognized intellect, eschewed public speaking. According to the Thomas Jefferson Encyclopedia, the third president was "not known as an outstanding orator." In fact, both of his inaugural addresses were barely audible. While the present State of the Union is delivered before members of Congress, Jefferson started a tradition in 1801, lasting many administrations, of not delivering such an address orally.[ii]

In one of my introductory courses in college, a professor suggested the main reason students drop out of a class is over the fear of speaking in front of their peers.

Confirming this assertion, the Chapman University Survey of America's Top Fears 2020/2021, found that 29 percent of Americans are afraid of public speaking. This means public speaking ranks higher than the fear of abduction (25.6 percent), walking alone at night (22.1 percent), and being murdered by a stranger (28.9 percent). Public speaking is evidently less scary than dying (29.3 percent), but not by much.[iii]

The range of public speaking fear is broad. Fear might manifest itself as small jitters or a shaky voice. You may have concerns about how the audience will perceive you, or you may have doubts about your expertise on a subject. You may simply not feel comfortable presenting yourself. You may feel awkward about your appearance, your mannerisms, and your language skills. You may worry incessantly before a planned speech or have an upset stomach during a meeting or class for fear of being recognized to speak. Some people become visibly nervous; some suffer sudden panic attacks.

For others, public speaking is a full anxiety-producing event that may eat away at a person's ability to function. If severe enough, it may be classified as a mental health issue or disorder.

While there may be comfort knowing you are not alone in these fears, there is perhaps more relief in understanding why they exist and what one can do about them. In a nutshell, it's all about you and how you view yourself and your circumstances.

Talk to the Cat

When I was a kid, I remember walking past my brother's bedroom and hearing him deep in conversation with someone. My brother was an incessant talker, which was a constant source of irritation to me. I discovered his conversation was with his favorite audience member—himself.

He was on to something. If you're hesitant to speak publicly, you need to get used to the sound of your own voice. Talk to yourself aloud while looking in the bathroom mirror (run the shower if you don't want anyone else to hear you). You don't have to say anything of importance; it can be as mundane as telling yourself what you had for dinner. Just speak and observe yourself doing it.

Give a prepared speech to your cat, or read a story to a stuffed bear. Talk out loud when you are in the middle of an activity. If you are baking cookies, speak the recipe and your actions: "Now I am taking out a large mixing bowl that will hold the dry ingredients, two cups of flour, two teaspoons of baking powder, a pinch of salt. I will stir for fifteen seconds." If you are mowing the lawn, make the same type of oration: "I am taking the lawn mower over to the corner of the yard, and then I will turn on the motor and mow in a horizontal pattern." The sound of your voice may startle you—that's good; get used to it.

Practice answering questions aloud when you're driving in the car alone. When I'm on an open highway, I often articulate speeches that I have written in my head. Trust me, no one cares if they see you talking to yourself while whizzing down the road at 60 mph. (Although there was a time that I was driving in downtown Washington, DC, with my windows and sunroof open, singing along loudly to a Sheryl Crow song. Stopped at a red light, I noticed the handsome man in the car next to me was looking over and smiling. I am a horrible, horrible singer. At first, I wanted to crawl under the steering wheel, but I decided to lean into it. I cranked up the radio and my singing and gave the man a wave.)

Simply listen to yourself speak. There's no pressure and no one is listening but you. These exercises will help you become more comfortable with the sound of your own voice. Think of it as going to the gym. Instead of lifting weights to add muscle tone to your arms, you're speaking aloud to add smoothness to your voice.

As you become accustomed to speaking aloud, focus less on your words and more on the person in front of you. When you speak to yourself in front of a mirror, you should be looking at you. Watch your reaction to your own words. Do you look calm, terrified, nervous, happy, bored? My guess is that you look rather comfortable, since it's only you and the mirror. You may find that after uttering only a few words in the mirror you suddenly sound a little anxious. It's as if you're thinking of all the things that might go wrong. Nonetheless, keep repeating the words aloud. The more you speak to it, the more you will instill a feeling of comfort.

Once you become comfortable speaking before an audience of one, it's time to expand your audience. Will your brother, sister, spouse, good friend, or classmate listen to you read from a page in a book or practice a full presentation? Select someone you trust to listen. When my brother was older, and far less annoying, I served as a sounding board for his professional presentations.

Sometimes it's more comfortable, and less personal, to try this exercise with someone you don't know very well. I like to try out new speeches by giving them to someone who knows little to nothing about the subject. It helps me focus on the clarity of the speech rather than its content. While a phrase might look good on paper, sometimes it doesn't translate when spoken aloud. I'll try out a section several times until it actually makes better sense to me and to those listening.

At what point do you become uncomfortable: when you speak to one person, two people, ten, or five hundred? Once you get comfortable reciting your speech in the mirror, the number of people eventually listening to you will not matter as much. Consider adding people gradually to your speaking circle to boost your confidence and help you realize you have a voice worth sharing.

Confidence building is a common theme for many public speakers. Keep in mind, US President Joe Biden grew up with a stutter, which he has called "debilitating." Yet he conquered that stutter by practicing for hours reading poetry in front of a mirror. CNN commentator Anderson Cooper, when interviewing then–presidential candidate Biden on February 5, 2020, revealed that his mother, the famed fashion designer Gloria Vanderbilt, also stuttered. A movie called *The King's Speech* tells the story of the well-known stutter of England's King George VI and the speech therapist who coached the king in delivering public addresses. None of these people let stuttering define their lives. They each worked through the condition in different ways.

You, too, can build the confidence needed to speak publicly.

Listen and Adjust

Another way to calm your nerves is to listen more intently to others. Listen to how your friends and colleagues speak. Do they stammer over certain words? Do they say "um" or "you know" or use other distracting filler words? Do they sometimes sound like they have no idea what they're talking about? Of course they do! You probably just haven't noticed because you're too concerned with your own speech insecurities.

These same friends and colleagues, no matter their faults, continue to give presentations and speak up publicly. You should too. Although we may strive for improvement, no one is perfect at speaking. Sure, someone may blow a speech out of the water, but speaking is an art form that's open to subjective critique.

Most people do not speak as though they are delivering a well-rehearsed TED Talk. When you listen to others—be they friends, colleagues or celebrities—pay attention to those speech qualities that you most admire and aim to emulate them.

Have you noticed how your favorite speakers might modulate the volume of their voice, or how they use seemingly elegant gestures? Do you admire someone who speaks off the cuff with passion? Do you enjoy how your favorite professor can make people laugh in the middle of a dull topic? Do you like the way a speaker seems to speak directly to you? Do you appreciate how they pause to add greater emphasis to a point?

I've been fortunate to receive invitations to many Stowell Lectures. The lecture series, named for Robert E. Stowell, MD, a distinguished pathologist and former president of the American Registry of Pathology, featured pioneers in investigative pathology, space medicine, paleopathology, and other scientific topics. Each speaker had their own style, but each lecture I attended was highly memorable and impactful because of how the speaker engaged others with their knowledge. It's a style I aim to emulate.

Often the most effective speaker isn't a famous person or a professional orator. Instead it's someone who has knowledge, passion, and confidence in the matter they discuss. I have listened to tens of thousands of speakers and I enjoy most hearing from someone who is earnest about their topic and natural in their delivery.

One way to become a more natural speaker is to eliminate nervous-sounding habits. To avoid using distracting filler words, you first need to realize that you actually say them. I am hypervigilant about noticing when people say "um" before, after, and in the middle of their sentences. It's distracting and lacks polish.

In the 1980s, a stereotype of a materialistic, self-absorbed young woman was referred to as a "valley girl." Valley girls had unique speech patterns. They would pepper their sentences with the words "like whatever" or "totally" or "um." These filler phrases would help them avoid a break in conversation and made them sound clueless as a result.

Speakers don't always realize they use the occasional "uh" and "um." Now that you are aware of these filler words, you'll start to hear them too. That's the first step in conquering this annoying speech habit. The second step is realizing that you have a different option for gathering your thoughts while speaking publicly. That option is to allow yourself a silent pause.

That's right; if you're having trouble finding the right word to use to express a thought, or if you simply forget where you are in your speech, stop talking. The first few times you try this it will seem to you like an eternity of silence! It's not. Taking a silent moment to gather your thoughts will actually keep people listening to you. They want to know what you will say next. Pausing for a few seconds will make you a more impressive speaker and help eliminate the fear of forgetting what to say.

By listening more intently, you will learn positive speaking techniques too. For example, a colleague of mine who is shy about speaking up at meetings once told me she liked that I started my reports by introducing the other people involved in the effort. She noticed two things about this approach: it paid respect to others; and it gave her time to become more comfortable in the room as she saw her colleagues welcomed and acknowledged.

Another technique is to ask your audience a question. If you are searching for a word, or you think you're losing the audience's attention, ask for their help. You might ask, "Is everyone with me so far?" or "What's that word?" or "How do you say . . .?"

Be Vulnerable

A technical manager I know had to deliver a fifteen-minute talk introducing himself and his program to a room of his organization's senior executives. He was petrified. There's no question he knows himself and his program cold, but standing in front of nine other people who were judging him was making him ill. He had no choice but to push through it. His next move was brilliant. He introduced himself by name and then, with a sickly pallor on his face, told the audience that public speaking was not "his thing" and it was truly terrifying to be there. He also said he wanted to learn and improve.

In that moment, he endeared himself to the group with his vulnerability, his ownership of his weakness, and his resolve to do better. One executive piped up and said, "Don't worry; we just want to hear what you have to say." The audience was rooting for him. By admitting his insecurities, it helped to erase them and ease his nervousness. His presentation was well received, and his work was acknowledged.

To face your public speaking fears, you can admit them to your audience to put everyone—including yourself—at ease.

Keep in mind that this is not a repeatable solution. Once you've told your boss, your colleagues, or your professor that giving a speech makes you nervous, it is incumbent upon you to improve your public speaking skills (like by reading this book!). It's really not an excuse you can use twice.

You can endear yourself to your audience by also telling them a little about yourself. You might explain your position within an organization: Are you a sophomore at Ellington High School or an account supervisor at Acme Corp? You may have experience to share that is relevant to your speech. If you give a talk on holiday shopping, tell the audience about your fourteen years of professional gift-wrapping experience. If you speak on time management techniques, explain how being a parent has helped you learn these skills.

Look at it this way. Which of the following speakers would you rather hear from?

"Hello, I'm Dr. Bruce Banner from Culver University, and I'm here to discuss gamma radiation with you today."

Or:

"Hello, I'm Dr. Bruce Banner from Culver University. I have seven doctoral degrees with expertise in gamma radiation, which we will discuss today. By the way, just so you know, when I get angry, my skin tends to take on a green hue. But don't worry; I'm really happy to be here."

The latter is obviously a much more inviting introduction. It reveals a little about the speaker and helps put the audience—and the speaker—at ease.

A note of caution, however: Do not overshare or try to be someone you are not. The audience, in this case, does not need to know that Dr. Bruce Banner was a fugitive from the US government or that he broke up with his girlfriend, Betty. You are not Dr. Banner or the Hulk, so leave that out of your talk too.

A friend of mine, Marcia Nusgart, is a well-known executive in the wound care industry. Hosting a major conference on the subject, Marcia was thinking of how to engage the audience with her opening remarks. Instead of the usual "we're so glad you're here today," Marcia shared a little bit about herself. She told the audience full of executives and policymakers that she got engaged last year (to which everyone cheered), but said that she's been too busy planning this stellar conference to worry about planning a wedding too. Throughout the professional conference, the audience was abuzz with the news and half expected a surprise walk down the aisle at the end.

Roll with It

Be prepared for the unexpected, and resolve yourself to adjust to the situation. US President Bill Clinton famously did just that in a speech to the nation on September 22, 1993. Standing before a joint session of Congress televised to millions of people, President Clinton was to deliver a speech that defined his health care agenda. As the welcoming applause died down and the president turned his attention to the teleprompter in front of him, he realized the text of the speech was wrong. Instead of his health care address, it was a different speech he had delivered months before. He had to wing it for several minutes while there was a behind-the-scenes scramble to correct the situation. Few were the wiser until the error was revealed after the address. To the audience, the president had appeared collected, calm, and on-message with his health care address.

One of President Clinton's chief aides, Paul Begala, was interviewed years later, in 2009, by Melissa Block on the program *All Things Considered*. Evidently, the situation was more trying than first reported. Mr. Begala explained that he had taken the president's glasses away from him and, "to save time," had printed the backup written copy in a small font type. He recounted: "So the poor guy was blind without his glasses, couldn't read 12-point type. And the teleprompter had the wrong speech whizzing a hundred miles an hour forward and backward around him." He asked the president what it felt like to stand "in front of the Congress of the United States, biggest speech of your life, technical topic, and have the teleprompter break." According to Mr. Begala, the president responded, "I thought, 'Well Lord, you're testing me. Okay, here goes.'"[iv]

Maybe you aren't planning to give an address to a joint session of Congress, but the lesson is the same. Be prepared for the unexpected. If you realize that something is unlikely to go exactly as planned, it can be less scary when your best planned speech has a glitch.

A glitch that flummoxed me happened at the University of Chicago. I had been invited to speak at a special symposium on health care. It was thrilling to receive an invitation from this venerable institution. Other panelists included a future director of the Centers for Disease Control and Prevention and top health care brass at the Department of Defense. This was not a speech to mess up.

The evening before the event, the speakers and our host got to know one another over a dinner table at a local restaurant. We exchanged stories, discussed plans for the symposium, and enjoyed the camaraderie. The next day, the same host introduced each of us before we spoke. I listened to the impressive talks of the other panelists. Then it was my turn. The host stood at the podium to introduce me, but I wasn't the one she called. She nodded toward me but said the wrong name. I don't mean she mispronounced my name; I mean I was not the person she thought I was. My affiliation was also noted incorrectly. She finished her introduction of me and the audience applauded while I made my way to the podium.

As I took those ten long steps, I weighed what to do. Do I correct, and likely embarrass, our host? Telling a joke about it might have embarrassed both her and me. Do I correct the host and then get booted from Chicago because I was the wrong person? Am I not the person they wanted to invite? I didn't know the person who was mentioned. Imposter syndrome is not a condition that ails me, but if it did, that moment would have been the opportune time to have an attack.

As mortified as I was, I decided to pretend the whole thing never happened. I recall thanking the host for the introduction, stating my real name and affiliation, and then just moving on. I didn't try to prove that I was the one invited to speak. The point of this recounting is that you can't plan for everything that will go wrong with your presentation. However, you can anticipate that something might, and just be prepared to function through it.

There are countless stories of interruptions that occur during speeches. Sir David Niven, an actor, was speaking at the Academy Awards in 1974, when a man streaked buck naked across the stage. Unflappable, the actor offered a clever retort: "Isn't it fascinating to think that probably the only laugh that man will ever get in his life is by stripping off and showing his shortcomings?" Interruptions occur with less global audiences too: People may enter the room loudly, a baby may cry, a cell phone may ring with a catchy tune. Depending on the circumstances, you might ignore it and keep talking, stop and let the interruption pass, or address it directly ("great ring tone!"). Life happens, yet your speech will go on.

US Representative Madeleine Dean once taught a lesson on how to be cool under pressure. Named a manager in the January 2021 presidential impeachment trial, Rep. Dean found herself interrupted by a senator's objection while standing at a podium delivering her closing statement before all 100 members of the United States Senate and a global virtual audience.

It was not entirely clear to the public what was happening, but defense attorneys and impeachment managers had approached the bench behind her to argue a point with staff. Rep. Dean stood to the side of the podium while this tense situation unfolded. Eventually, with the matter resolved, she returned to the podium, took a breath, and said calmly, "I have to say that, of all the trials I have ever been a part of, this is certainly one of them." It eased the tension and focused the audience back on her and her closing remarks.

Make Friends

Another way to ease your nerves when delivering a speech is by befriending others in the room. You don't have to be best chums, but arrive early to get to know a few people prior to your talk. Whether sitting around a conference room table or speaking to a theater of hundreds, introducing yourself to the person sitting next to you helps to develop some familiarity between you and your upcoming audience.

It's easy to walk into an auditorium or conference room and pull out your smartphone to check your messages before speaking. Don't do it. This is an opportune time to connect with the people around you. Give them your name and ask for theirs. Ask what brings them to the conference. Ask what they hope to learn from the speakers. You might find that you'll be able to address many of the issues they raise when it's your turn to present. Most of all, you'll develop a rapport with audience members in advance, quelling any nerves you may have.

If you will be joined by other speakers or know who else will be in the room, do some homework to learn more about their background or the topic on which they may be speaking.

Are other speakers listed on LinkedIn? Ask to connect with them by saying that you will both be presenting on the same panel. This is a way to get to know others before even entering the room.

Have they spoken on the topic previously? If so, you may be able to watch one of their speeches on YouTube or another online source. You don't have to become an expert on your colleagues, but understanding what they do and their interests may put you at ease.

What is their position on a specific topic? If you will be speaking to a task force or committee, it will benefit you to understand what others think on the matter. This will help you realize who may be most supportive of what you have to say.

Is there a welcoming event? Try to participate in any hospitality event that precedes your talk. It's another opportunity to become familiar with who will be in the audience when you speak. Be sure to wear your name tag, if the meeting provides one, so others may learn who you are.

If you'll be speaking from a stage or at a podium, take a moment to learn who is responsible for the meeting production or who is on the technical crew. These people want the meeting to proceed without a glitch. They can help you feel more comfortable by acquainting you with the room. If you arrive early enough, you may have an opportunity to do a sound check with the microphone or get hooked up with a lavalier. They will show you where the projector, screen, and cameras may be located. You'll learn how to adjust the height of the podium, if used. If you show up exactly in time for your talk, or when there is a queue of people in front of you, there will be less of an opportunity for the production crew to assist you in becoming familiar with these useful details.

You're an Investment

As you work on tackling your fear, remember that you matter. Someone is invested in you and what you plan to say.

This is true whether you are in a public speaking competition where your coach, your teammates, and the judges are there to support you, or you are speaking before a large business conference where people have paid an admission fee because they want to hear your words of wisdom.

People listen to others speak for many different reasons. Some want to learn about the subject matter, some listen to have their own opinions validated, a few want to network with others, and some may have only heard your name but think you may be interesting. I've attended plenty of meetings where I just wanted to hear what an obscure CEO of a new technology start-up was working on or to understand what an up-and-coming artist was thinking in creating a sculpture. Of course, others only came for the cake served after the talk, but there'll be no sweets unless they listen first.

One of my college professors taught US government. He was also a renowned political pollster. I absolutely loved the subject matter, but the class bored me. The professor would assign chapters to read, then teach on that same material in class. He would ask many questions, but often would not call on the students who raised their hands to be recognized. Instead, he called on the students who apparently did not read the chapter the night before, which was the vast majority of the class.

I was determined to get some value out of these lectures, so I concocted a game. When the professor asked a question that I didn't feel like answering, I raised my hand. When I wanted to discuss a subject, or provide a direct answer, I did not raise my hand. The professor called on me every time my hand was in my lap.

It's not the best way to get an education, but I really wanted to learn from this professor when he spoke. I was invested in his words, but had to figure out how to get a better rate of return. The same is true for many public speeches. Every word you utter may not be golden, but the audience is invested in what you have to say.

Chapter Two

Set Your Style

The Washington Ideas Forum was an annual event sponsored by the *Atlantic* and the Aspen Institute. This well-crafted, two-day affair was filled with in-person interviews with prominent newsmakers and journalists, opportunities to network with serious-minded policy wonks, and the coolest snack bars filled with color-arranged candies and other goodies. The 2014 event was no exception. The alluring stage was set to receive Craig Venter, founder, chairman and chief executive officer of the J. Craig Venter Institute; Eric Holder, US attorney general; Catherine Mohr, vice president of medical research at Intuitive Surgical; Jim McKelvey, co-founder of Square; Walter Isaacson, president of the Aspen Institute; Mia Burk, president of Alta Planning + Design; Anthony Fauci, director of the National Institute of Allergy and Infectious Diseases; Chimamanda Ngozi, author of *Americanah*; John Kerry, US secretary of state; David Rubenstein, co-founder and co-chief executive officer of the Carlyle Group; and many others. I linked arms with a former US senator, chatted about international affairs with agency officials, and connected with others on health policy issues. Yet after all these years, the most memorable moment of the event came from then-Secretary of Commerce Penny Pritzker. She wore a killer outfit.

In an attractive knit skirt and top, Secretary Pritzker exuded a modern, comfortable professionalism. I wanted to ask her where she shopped. While that line of questioning may have been appropriate for my personal commerce purposes, it had nothing to do with economic growth and opportunity for the country. I never asked the question of the head of the US commerce department.

How you present yourself matters in public speaking. This includes your appearance, your temperament, and your actions. Whether we like it or not, people judge each other on these nonverbal components of a presentation.

Let's be clear. You do not need to look like Zendaya, Michael B. Jordan, Christie Brinkley, or George Clooney to be confident in speaking up publicly. You do not need a wrinkle-free forehead, ripped abs, or toned legs. You do not need designer clothing, sunglasses, or an attitude.

You need to be you—the best version of you.

Wear a Killer Outfit

While competing in high school forensics we had rituals, some may call them superstitions, that made us more comfortable. As soon as someone won a tournament, whatever they were wearing at the time became their competition "uniform." Yes, some people took it to the extreme—lucky blazer, lucky shoes, lucky underwear—but if it worked, it worked.

The point is to set the right appearance. Do you feel good in what you are wearing? Put some thought into your outfit. Does it fit properly? Is it appropriate for the occasion?

As chair of a local government subcommittee, I was asked to make an official statement at a public hearing. I wore a red linen jacket with matching pleated skirt and a taupe scoop-neck shirt. I liked the outfit and thought it appropriate for the setting. I gave my televised presentation at the podium and went back to sit in the front row. Something felt odd. I looked down and noticed my skin-colored, bulky shoulder pad had come loose and lodged itself on top of my left breast. At first, I was embarrassed, but soon started giggling to myself. I gingerly placed my hand over my heart while keeping my eyes on the faces of the elected officials. Did they notice? I grabbed the shoulder pad and stuffed it in my purse. Life happens. Thankfully no one commented on my lopsided buxomness. Let's just hope no one finds the archival tape.

Before your speech or meeting begins, take a moment to look in the mirror. While your shoulder pad may not be hanging by a thread at that particular time, you will feel more confident if you know your hair is in place, your fly is zipped, and your teeth are free of spinach. It's not necessary to wear a designer label or the latest shoes, but your clothes should fit you. If your pants are falling off your hips, put on a belt. If your shirt is sheer, add something over or under it.

There is often an atmosphere of "anything goes" when it comes to clothing. It's a mistake to assume it will have no impact on your speech.

Take the founder and chief executive of Facebook, Mark Zuckerberg, who became known for not only his enterprise mastery, but also his jeans, gray t-shirts, and hoodies. Mountains of articles and social media posts have speculated about his clothing choices. Yet wearing jeans and a t-shirt to testify before Congress is considered disrespectful of the institution. When he testified publicly, even Zuckerberg wore a suit and tie.

I hesitantly bought an expensive black sweater replete with holes, tears and snags. Yes, how au courant of me. I do wear it out socially, but in truth, it looks like I'm sporting a sweater that got tugged out of a dumpster. If I were a 5'11" fashion model, maybe I could pull it off at a public presentation, but

I'm not. Wearing it to a public speaking event would only have folks whispering that I was a mess.

There is a saying "clothes make the man." It sounds like an advertising pitch, but the idiom has been expressed for centuries and across cultures. Dr. Nancy Micklewright's article, "Clothes Make the Man," published in volume 47 of *Ars Orientalis*, explains, "(A)s Shakespeare wrote in Hamlet, 'The apparel oft proclaims the man.'" She cited similar sentiments from other cultures, including Egypt ("dressing up a stick turns it into a doll") and Korea ("Clothes are wings"). Appropriate attire is universal.

What you wear is a reflection of who you are and how you want to be perceived.

If you're speaking at a trade show and most people are wearing khakis and short-sleeved polo shirts with their company's name embossed over the breast pocket, then it's fine to wear the same for your talk. If you're the keynote speaker at a formal, black-tie event, then an evening gown or tuxedo would be more suitable than a blazer. If you are unsure of the customs at your event, don't hesitate to ask one of the organizers who should be able to share if the event dress is business casual, business suit, semi-formal, or formal.

You can accessorize your outfit to personalize your appearance. A brightly colored scarf may perk up a conservative dress. A pair of patterned socks may bring a little flair to a business suit. A fashion necklace may add a statement to a plain shirt. Just make certain these embellishments don't distract from what you want to say. A fun pair of oversized hoop earrings or a dangling charm bracelet may be your favorites, but they likely will jingle as you speak—a no-no.

Not everyone is attuned to their appearance, which can lead to unintended consequences. Years ago, the US House of Representatives considered legislation that would cut Medicare physician reimbursement rates significantly. A trade association advocating against those cuts had many valid arguments on their side. Those economic arguments were undermined when congressional staff saw association leaders arrive on Capitol Hill in a stretch limo.

Similarly, an individual wearing a Rolex watch and Louboutin heels to speak about hunger is sending a mixed message to a food bank audience. On the flip side, wearing cargo pants and a sweatshirt makes a poor sartorial statement if you wear them to present at a conference of senior executives.

It doesn't mean you can't wear what you want. You may certainly wear a t-shirt and jeans when presenting at a conference, or before a committee, or at a forensics tournament, but should you? It helps to think about your appearance and the circumstances of your talk.

The same goes for virtual meetings when you speak publicly. You should consider the cyberspace an extension of the meeting. Ditch the pajama tops and wear something that will help you exude confidence and professionalism.

A friend of mine worked for nearly twenty years with a man who always wore a suit and tie to work. His presence at meetings was revered, not just for the content of his speech, but for the professional way he dressed and carried himself. Once the COVID-19 pandemic hit, meetings went virtual. This same man, who never varied his conduct in those twenty years, was suddenly giving presentations in his sweats. His hair was no longer neatly combed, it was tousled. My friend remarked that while this man's words were still valuable, he came across as a less influential person.

No matter the platform, appearances register with the audience. Take the time to plan your outfits accordingly.

Build Your Body

I once attended a talk given by a well-known actress and film producer who was introduced as someone who "has always shown us the power of imperfection and the crucial nature of mistakes." This preface was right on the mark. As she was interviewed in front of hundreds of fans, the accomplished star could not stop fidgeting with her long hair. She would sweep it behind her right ear, then her left ear, then she would flip it over her shoulder, and then toss it to the opposite shoulder. These were constant movements throughout her talk. I stopped listening and thought about how I wanted to run up on stage with a pair of scissors to chop off her locks.

How you present yourself physically has an impact, no matter how famous or experienced you are.

Another common public speaking fidget involves pockets. Some people place a hand in the pocket of their trousers or dress thinking it exudes coolness or confidence. For some, it's just a comfortable place to rest their hand. All too often, placing your hand in a pocket while giving a speech leads to the clinking of coins or other movements that distract the audience to focus inappropriately on your pocket.

Just don't put your hands in your pockets. If it's a bad habit you can't seem to kick, make sure you remove coins, keys, and anything else that might jingle. So, what should you do with your hands, you ask? Just like a police officer may yell to a suspect, "Keep your hands where I can see them."

Here are a few tips on hand placement and gestures:

Build a box. Draw an imaginary red box in front of you. The top of the box should be chest level just below your shoulders. The bottom should be at your waist. The sides of box should be just a few inches wider than your shoulders. Your hands should fit comfortably within the red outlines of the box when you make a presentation.

Speak with your hands. Your gestures may be used to emphasize parts of your talk. For example, if you are making three points in your talk, use your index finger to show point number one, then two fingers to preface your second point, and three fingers for your final point. If you are comparing or contrasting separate issues, your gestures should follow along. For example, if giving a talk on gardening, use your right hand to say, "on the one hand, we will examine the benefits of planting perennials." Then, use your left hand when you explain, "as an alternative, we will examine the positive attributes of annual plants." All these gestures should be made within the imaginary box, so the audience will see them.

Idle time. If you are not making a point, keep your arms by your side or simply bend your arms to a ninety-degree angle and let your hands rest at waist level. Do not cross your arms against your chest; it closes you off to the audience.

Chill. Unless you are trying to make a forceful point, do not make a fist with your hands. For some people, it's natural to hold their hands in a fist position. To an audience, it will look like you are angry. An open hand generates warmth and trust.

Watch the Grammys. Yes, this sounds like an odd tip, but it can be fascinating to watch how professional singers handle their hand and arm movements. No, you need not adopt JLo's dance moves into your formal business talk (although good for you if you can). You will however notice what these stellar performers, standing at a microphone, do with their free hands. Some use their hands to add expression to an emotional moment. Others look as if they have a stiff, mechanical arm that someone coached to raise up and down. It's worth a look.

Your posture is important too. "Stand up straight" is not only a phrase your grandparents may have used, it's an important tool for conveying confidence and authority. If you slouch while speaking, you may look withdrawn and disinterested. To remedy a slouch, practice reading aloud pages from a book while balancing another book on your head. The book on your head will force you, whether you are standing or sitting, to straighten your back and use your eyes—not your shoulders—to glance downward at the pages to read.

If your shoulders are hunched over, your chin tucked down, and head bowed, you will appear less self-assured. You will likely feel less confident too. Remember to keep your shoulders back, chin up, and your head facing forward.

Then there's the matter of your feet. Notice how you're standing when you are about to speak. It's likely that your feet are facing forward, or maybe slightly off plumb, and about shoulder-width (or less) apart. If you are comfortable and not distracting in your movements, you should be just fine. I usually stand with my feet pointed in a somewhat modified "v" shape, which is somewhat similar to a ballerina's very relaxed, fourth-position pose.

There are variations on foot positioning that may draw unwanted attention to your feet. There is a cowhand stance with feet spaced so far apart that your body will look as if it's expecting a freight train to run under it. Or, I have seen dancers speak quite naturally while standing in a first-position ballet pose, where their heels almost touch and their toes face out sideways. If you're speaking on ranch matters or on the artistry of ballet, go for it. Everyone else might aim for a less distracting position.

It's perfectly acceptable to stand planted in one spot while you talk. It's also okay to move. There are limits to both. If you tend to pace back and forth while speaking, the audience may get motion sickness. Some people stand in one spot, but sway their bodies constantly, which can also induce nausea in your listeners. If you are giving a talk on the discomforts of sailing, this stance may reinforce your point. Chances are it's a nervous habit that you need to kick.

I pace when practicing a speech but slow down considerably when I have a real audience. If you want to move your feet while giving a presentation, aim to be purposeful in your steps. You might inch forward to get closer to the audience, or just move to appear less rigid.

Consider these tips for the feet.

Position your feet naturally. How do you stand when you look relaxed? Your feet are likely spaced no more than shoulder-width apart. Aim to use the same pose while delivering a speech.

Take baby steps. If you're hesitant to move, take just a step or two either to the side or toward the audience. Then, work from that new spot until you are ready to move another couple of steps. Don't step backward; it will look as if you are retreating.

Crossing your legs. If you are giving a talk while seated, you still need to think about your feet positioning. The circumstances behind this tip vary, as too will the response. For example, if you are wearing a short skirt while sitting on a pedestal chair on an elevated stage, then crossing your legs comes with some risk of revealing too much. In this instance, it's best to sit with your legs and knees together. If you're seated closely to other speakers on a panel, spreading your legs widely may appear uncouth. Likewise, entwining your legs with the legs of the chair is distracting and will make you appear nervous. Some people prefer to cross their legs or their ankles, and that's okay. However, the recommendation is to sit with your legs together and feet on the ground. You will look prepared, organized, and competent.

A podium will often be offered for formal presentations. I don't like them. To me, a podium creates a barrier between you and the audience. It's more relatable to speak without a wooden box in front of you. Yet there are circumstances where there will be little choice but to use one. If you are speaking at a college graduation or before a county council, everyone will use the podium.

I was invited to speak at a scientific conference. There were about fifty people in the audience in a room that was arranged in a classroom style with tables and chairs. When I arrived, I found a podium front and center with a wide, full-length easel behind it. The easel displayed prominently the names of certain advertisers. The hosts did not ask approval for filming my presentation, and I had zero interest in being associated with the unvetted advertisers. Standing behind a podium for such an intimate crowd seemed too distanced. I stepped to the side of the podium, outside of camera range, and spoke directly to the audience. The point is, I did not confine myself to an uncomfortable spot; I moved and made it my own. This likely did not please the hosts or the advertisers, but that wasn't my concern. The audience was interested and engaged.

Even with a podium, you need to be aware of your movements. The audience will still be able to see if you are hunched over, rocking nervously, or twirling your hair. Some speakers may feel more at ease with the podium barrier, but it does not alleviate the need to use mannerisms more effectively or to control apprehension.

If you do use a podium, be aware of your grip. It's okay to place your hands on either side of the podium, but try not to clasp it so hard that the wood stain rubs off on your palms. You may also place your hands in front of you and use your fingers to follow your written speech. Ideally, you will still gesture with your hands and arms at appropriate points during your talk.

The Eyes Have It

My grandmother has been blind for half of her life. She doesn't "look blind," meaning there is no outward clue for a

sighted person to realize instantly she cannot see. My glamorous grandmother, who with her striking good looks has often
been mistaken for a movie star, usually does not use her white
cane in public. Her eyes sparkle even though there is no light
coming in. She is radiant, and she radiates that warmth.

But far too often, when people discover she cannot see,
they stop talking to her directly. She can be holding an engaging conversation, but once the blindness factor is recognized,
people will turn their attention to the sighted person next to
her. Many times, others have asked me a question that should
have been directed to her. We both knew what was happening.
I would channel them back to my grandmother.

These awkward circumstances apply to public speaking as
well. If you don't acknowledge someone who is right in front
of you, why should they pay attention to you?

A 2013 study in the *Journal of Neuroscience* by Nicolas
Burra, et al., supports what my grandmother has experienced:
"The amygdala response to eye contact does not require an in-
tact primary visual cortex." In other words, the brain processes
eye contact even when the patient is blind. The authors determined that "direct gaze possesses an important behavioral
value . . . and is likely to constitute a powerful signal" even
without visual awareness.[v]

Yes, even if someone is blind, they know if they are being
seen. You, as the speaker, must strive to acknowledge your
audience. This is where eye contact comes into play.

Whether you are trying to persuade or merely tell a story,
making direct eye contact with your audience will help engage
them. It will make you appear more confident and trustworthy.
Just consider, if someone approached you on the street and
glanced furtively side-to-side without looking at you directly,
you'd think the person was rather shady. Direct eye contact
helps people understand and empathize with your words. Sure,
there will be plenty of people checking messages on their

phone or catching a few winks in some dimly lighted conference room, but the more you engage with them through your
eyes, the more compelled they will be to listen.

In Washington, DC, where I work and play, there is no
shortage of public encounters. Every day you witness visitors
meeting an elected official for the first time. Beforehand, it's
not unusual for the visitor to tell you how much they despise
senator A or representative B. Yet once they experience that
first eye-to-eye greeting, most visitors find that the politician
isn't so bad after all. Most elected officials are masters at
making eye contact when they speak.

When you look at your audience, you will also receive clues
about your presentation. If people are furrowing their eyebrows, maybe they don't understand something you just said.
Recognizing this expression allows you to take a moment to
explain further. You might pause and say, "Let me say that another way . . ." or "It's a challenging statement, but I'll explain
it in more detail momentarily."

If people like what you're saying, or agree with your point,
they may nod in the affirmative. Using your eyes will help you
realize you have support. You might even acknowledge the
subtle feedback by stating, "I see a lot of people nodding their
heads, I'm glad to see we are in sync."

Eye contact got me an "A" in a high school English class. My
family moved when I was in the middle of my freshman year
of high school. On my first day in a new school, there was one
seat left in Mrs. Carr's English class and it was the dreaded
front and center. I soon became thankful for that hot spot.

Mrs. Carr, a genteel person, had a wicked southern accent.
I had just spent several years up north and wasn't used to
her cadence or pronunciations. Honestly, I couldn't understand most of what she said. The class was in the middle of
Shakespeare's *Romeo and Juliet*, which fortunately I had already studied. I spent the rest of ninth-grade English intently

watching and lip-reading Mrs. Carr. It was the only way I knew what she said.

I never told anyone about my handicap. At the end of the semester, Mrs. Carr wrote a note: "Robin, you are the most attentive student!" Eye contact matters.

Making eye contact does not mean looking just above the heads of the audience to focus on a spot on the back wall. Nor does it mean lip-reading or staring down each person one by one. There is a happy, comfortable medium. There are several suggestions for getting started.

See a positive reflection. Take a moment to look yourself in the eyes in front of a mirror. Talk to yourself while holding the gaze. Get comfortable with looking at you.

Start slow. Making eye contact can be the most anxiety-producing aspect of public speaking, but it is an activity that gets easier over time. While gathering with a small group of your friends, see if you can determine the color of their eyes. There's no need to announce this experiment ahead of time, nor should you get up close and personal to find the answer. Once this personal experiment yields results, add others to the mix. Are you able to determine the eye color of your co-workers just by glancing at them? If so, you are making eye contact.

Three Mississippis. Eye contact does not mean burning the corneas of your audience members. Making contact for too long a period of time can be uncomfortable to your listener. Use the "Three Mississippis" rule as you work on this skill. When making eye contact with someone in the audience, your gaze should last no longer than three seconds ("One Mississippi, two Mississippi, three Mississippi"). It may be tough to juggle the real-time counting of Mississippis in your head while making your presentation. This reality brings us to the next tip.

A gaze for a sentence. As your skills improve, use your speech to dictate how long you make eye contact. For example, for every sentence you utter, look at one member of the audience and then move to another person for the next sentence. As you improve, you will be able to gauge how long to look at each person. A sentence may eventually become a paragraph or the completion of a thought.

Develop a pattern. After making eye contact with one audience member (back to the "Three Mississippis"), shift your attention slowly to another person in the room. This should be a natural movement. If you have one hundred people in the room, you will not have time to make eye contact with each person individually. Yet as you smoothly look to people around the room, you will be creating a rapport with them. One way to achieve this goal is to imagine the letter "R" hovering over the audience. You might start your talk by looking at the person at the bottom left of the letter; then move your gaze upward to the top of the letter; then across the top; down midway; then back to the left and diagonally down the room to the person sitting in the front on the right. With the letter "R" your eye gaze will look more natural and encompassing of the room.

Gain X-ray vision superpowers. Even when you become a pro at making eye contact during a speech, your listeners will not always be as savvy. Some audience members will never look at you; some will appear disinterested. Some may be as anxious as you may be and will avoid glancing your way. You need to keep talking and maintain eye contact regardless. Sometimes by looking at someone directly, you will actually command their attention (that's the superpower).

This last tip is one I mention often when preparing speakers to testify before Congress. Speaking before a congressional committee can terrify even the most confident of experts. There are many rules and traditions to observe. That's in addition to actually making your presentation. When the subject matter is complex, comprehensive, and sometimes arcane, that's a tough job to juggle.

To make matters worse, members of Congress may come and go during your talk. On Capitol Hill, that's not considered rude, it's regular conduct. You may be asked questions by the members of Congress, but you may have only seconds to respond. The person asking the question may appear disinterested in your answer. It can be nerve-wracking. A key to making it through successfully is to maintain eye contact with the seated panel members. You will appear confident and prepared, no matter the circumstances surrounding you.

Smile

In middle school, a kid named Christy came up to me with an ultimatum. "Stop smiling or I won't be friends with you anymore," she demanded. Now granted, I smile a lot. Why shouldn't I?

According to twelve-year-old Christy, it was a bad idea. I had lots of friends and wasn't particularly concerned about this threat, but it did give me pause. Was she offering wise advice, was she jealous, or was it just adolescent nonsense? I don't know, but I told her I liked smiling and she continued to be my friend a couple days later.

Christy's dour preference is the exception.

Smiling projects confidence. It says you're approachable. When you walk into a room or on to a stage to speak, enter with a smile on your face. It will put both you and the audience in a positive frame of mind. Frankly, even if you aren't feeling confident, a smile can trick you into believing it anyway. Smiling is contagious.

You don't have to deliver a big toothy grin, if that isn't you. If you can muster only a little curvature of your mouth, that's fine. Some people prefer to smile with their eyes, crinkling their eyes to convey a positivity.

If you wear a perpetual frown or just find no reason to smile, try this trick. Practice holding a number two pencil in your teeth. Your pencil bite will perpetuate a smile. Take a look in the mirror when you do it and see if you can emulate this look, minus the pencil, when you speak.

Another way to coerce a smile is to think a pleasant thought or remind yourself of a funny joke or situation. You don't have to be doubled over in fits of laughter, just try not to appear with a sour look on your face. Greet the audience with an expression that is warm and approachable.

When Smiling Doesn't Fit

When delivering speeches on somber topics or conveying devastating news, a happy smile may not fit the circumstances. Yet you still want the audience to trust and engage with you. Moments in history illustrate how this is accomplished. President Ronald Reagan addressed the nation on January 28, 1986, about the devastating explosion of the Challenger space shuttle. His introductory manner was calm yet forceful, soothing yet blunt, and his expression, while somber, was warm.

After the tragic 2018 shooting at Marjory Stoneman Douglas High School in Parkland, Florida, thousands of people gathered in Washington, DC for a "March for Our Lives" rally. A student, Emma Gonzalez, spoke about her friends that were killed. She explained how no one was untouched by the violence and that it may be difficult to comprehend the extent of the heartbreak and devastation. She then stood silent for six minutes and twenty seconds to signify the time it took the killer to carry out his rampage. It was a powerful statement.

When leading with a speech on a tragic or somber occasion, you may express anger, hurt, and grief, but to be most effective, lead with dedication and purpose in your voice.

I first met the civil rights icon, US Representative John Lewis, at a small gathering near Capitol Hill where he spoke of his personal experiences in the civil rights movement. Forthright in his manner, Rep. Lewis described the struggles he endured, including being beaten bloody and suffering a fractured skull while crossing the Edmund Pettis Bridge in Selma, Alabama in 1965. Growing up, he had wanted to be a minister and practiced preaching to his family's chickens. He went on to deliver many poignant speeches including one at the Lincoln Memorial in 1963. He recited the traumatizing events—both the personal and societal injustices alike—in a plain, composed manner. His words and calmness were touching. Meeting with him personally afterward, I started to cry.

When you can't smile with your mouth, smile with your heart. People will hear you.

Other Facial Expressions

Public presentations may awaken a range of emotions. Acknowledging these emotions through facial expressions gives depth to your presentation. Your face does not have to register only in a single, stoic mode. If you say something funny, it's okay to laugh along. If you are conveying a sad tale, your face and voice may bear that sorrow. If you are presenting a confusing situation, it's okay to furrow your brow while explaining the conundrum to your audience.

In short, it's okay to be human.

Show anger on your face, if warranted. A nonprofit corporation in my town specializes in developing affordable housing complexes. Because home affordability is a high community priority and there is little competition for this service, some leaders tend to treat this corporation with kid gloves. Moldy, rat-infested apartment units and unmet-promises had gone unchecked for years. When speaking publicly about these conditions, a wink and a smile would be wholly inappropriate and insulting to those affected by the apparent negligence. Your expression should meet the situation.

You can roll your eyes if you say something incredulous. President Reagan mildly uttered the phrase "There you go again" when countering an opponent's statement in 1980. A slight eye roll here could be used with aplomb. Yet remember there is a line between creating skepticism and making a mockery. An effective public speaker should not taunt others with eye rolls and rude gestures.

Watch for expressions that may convey the wrong message. Biting your lip might show that you are worried or stressed. Covering your mouth with your hand can give the impression that you have something to hide—perhaps you do. If you are laughing or smirking at someone, you might be tempted to cover it up. Or maybe you are signaling to the audio crew that the microphone should be turned up and you don't want the audience to hear the instruction. That's fine, but the audience will wonder what you're doing.

I gave a eulogy years ago for a dear cousin. For the most part, I told funny stories of the times we spent together. Despite the sad occasion, I smiled when recounting these situations. The stories helped to console his immediate family, so smiling was appropriate and welcomed.

Pitch Perfect

If you had to draw a picture of a stereotypical southern sorority girl, you might describe Frances. Frances was a proud, lovely, and petite member of Chi Omega or maybe it was Tri Delta. She had pale white skin, volumes of blond hair, and a thick, honeyed accent. Unlike her stereotype, she was a studious, "A" undergrad, and wanted to improve her presentation skills. To do so, she joined the ragtag college forensics team.

Frances labored on her speech and faithfully practiced before competitions. Her talk was on services for the blind, a passionate subject for her.

After her first out-of-state competition, the team piled into the van to head back to campus. The coach handed out our critique slips, which we took turns reading aloud. As everyone was looking over their evaluations, there was a loud shriek from the back of the van. Frances was crying, "I don't understand, I don't understand!"

Her judge's assessment was blistering. It read something to the effect of, "How could you say these things about Black people? This talk is highly offensive and serves to highlight your ignorance and prejudice."

Frances muttered, "I'm not prejudiced! What does he mean? I didn't even talk about race!" It didn't take us long to decipher the issue: Her accent got in the way of her presentation. When she said the word "blind," the judge heard the word "black."

So, when Frances discussed disabilities and technologies to assist blind people in crossing a street, the judge heard her talk about Black people.

We couldn't stop laughing. Yes, given what the judge heard, her speech was highly offensive, but it wasn't what she said. Frances' confusion turned to mortification. It encouraged her to practice all the more and improve her speaking skills.

Voice and enunciation matter. You don't need to erase your accent, but you do need to speak clearly and smoothly enough for others to understand you.

During puberty, male voices can noticeably crack or sound broken as they change. It's all part of the natural process of growing, but it can sound awkward. Eventually, those teen and pre-teen voices even out. Giving a speech at this stage of life is just fine and sometimes you can work in the awkward squeaks. In the 1970s television show, *The Brady Bunch*, the middle son character, Peter, was experiencing his voice change. The show incorporated his voice modulations into a song called "Time to Change."

Voice swings are not just a pubescent matter.

Some people struggle to find the right pitch at which to speak. I have especially heard young women with high octave voices struggling to speak in an even manner. Their voices sound nervous or squeaky because they are not speaking at their natural pitch and range. One way to train yourself to identify your natural pitch is to hum in a quiet room. This is not the time to chant along to your favorite song, rather just making a humming sound with your voice. As you hear yourself, add some words into that hum. You might hum, "I am on the phone." Keep repeating those words until you eventually eliminate the hum and just say the words, "I am on the phone." This should be your natural speaking level. Work on speaking at this range and see if you feel more relaxed with your voice.

You should also avoid speaking in a questioning manner. Sometimes when nerves or uncertainty hit, a speaker will turn all sentences into questions, raising their volume and inflection at the end of each sentence. This style exposes to the audience the speaker's naivete and calls into question the authenticity of their comments.

Think of it this way. A police captain speaks before a citizens group on public safety matters. Which statement below is more authoritative, informative, and comforting?

Example A

There have been a rash of break-ins in the Azalea Wood neighborhood last week. The perpetrators appear to be accessing homes through unlocked doors and open garages. Items stolen have included bicycles, toolkits, and televisions. Please remember to lock your doors and conduct nightly security checks. If you hear noises or see something unfamiliar, please contact the police department at 123-456-7890.

Or:

Example B

There have been a rash of break-ins in the Azalea Wood neighborhood last week? The perpetrators appear to be accessing homes through unlocked doors and open garages? Items stolen have included bicycles, toolkits, and televisions? Please remember to lock your doors and conduct nightly security checks? If you hear noises or see something unfamiliar, please contact the police department at 123-456-7890?

Example A, read without the question marks or voice swings, is more authoritative than example B, where it appears the captain is unsure of which week, neighborhood, entry point, and phone number are correct. The surest way of addressing this voice issue is to become aware of it. Once you or a trusted colleague notices you swing your sentence tone upward, it's easier to control this annoying habit.

Here are some other tips for leveling your voice and enunciation before a presentation.

Hydrate. Your vocal cords vibrate more than a hundred times per second when you speak. Water helps to lubricate those cords, giving you a clearer sound. Drinking water throughout the day is a good practice, and taking a sip before a talk is especially helpful.

No ice. Room temperature water is best for your voice before and during a speech. Besides, who wants to deal with clinking ice cubes when you're speaking.

Don't clear your throat. You may tend to clear your throat when it's dry or you have a tickle, but it makes matters worse. It grinds your vocal cords, giving you a scratchy voice. Water here too is the answer (or good allergy medication, if your healthcare provider says so). Instead of straining to clear your throat, drink some water. If your throat still feels clogged, try a gentle, silent cough with an open mouth. This will help to blow away the feeling of obstruction.

No soda. Caffeinated soda—despite all the great thirst-quenching commercials—adds to dehydration (a no-no). Whether scientifically proven or not, soda may also temporarily lower your pitch, implying a vocal strain. Eliminating the drink may be one of those family remedies that generations of speakers pass down to one another, but it's worth a listen.

Sure, you may not be convinced to give up soda before a talk, but consider this life hack for cleaning a corroded car battery. Spritz cola on to the corroded parts and watch it eat away at the rust. Your vocal cords should not be as shiny!

For those of you who cannot function without a liter of caffeinated soda each day, at least wash down that drink with an equal volume of water. It will help lessen the damage.

Oohing and aahing. This may seem strange, but it worked wonders for the students I coached. Before every forensics competition, we would find an empty room, close the door, and loudly recite various sounds that begin with vowels: "Aaaaaah-hhh," "eeeeeee," "iiiiiiiiiiiiiiii," "ooohhh," "uuuuuuu," and then we'd get fancy with "aaaapppp," "eeeeppp," "oooopppp," 'ooom-mmm," and other combinations. The sounds were best accompanied by wide, exaggerated mouth movements. Yes, it was weird. No, everyone was not thrilled with these exercises at first. But the nervousness in our voices was eliminated and it was a great team-building warm-up. Now, when I'm by myself before a big speech, I still like to limber-up this way. If circumstances don't permit it, I take a few deep breaths instead.

Blow bubbles. Use your mouth to blow air through a straw into a glass of water. You may have been scolded for doing this as a child, but it's actually therapeutic before a speech. There's even a technical term for it—straw phonation.

Loosen up. Relax your shoulders and neck by raising your shoulders up toward your ears and then releasing them. Repeat several times. Tilt your head to the right, lower it in front of your body and then raise it to the left. Repeat this pendulum motion several times.

Stop talking. Larry Hagman, the actor who played Major Nelson on *I Dream of Jeannie* and J.R. Ewing on the night time soap opera *Dallas*, had a rule of silence on Sundays at his home.[vi] You don't have to go to this extreme, but saving your voice before a big speech is not a bad idea.

Practice those regional words. If it's difficult for others to understand you because of an accent, identify the most troubling words. My Spanish language professor in college admitted he had a tough time during spring break when many students wanted to go to the beach. When he spoke in English with his Cuban accent, "beach" became "bitch": "Myrtle Bitch," "Miami Bitch." He realized it was an English word that required some mastery.

Straining your voice is a relatively common phenomenon. According to the National Institute on Deafness and Other Communication Disorders (NIDCD), almost eighteen million Americans reported problems with their voice. I'm one of them. Despite my enjoyment with public speaking, I'm considered rather soft-spoken. I hear me just fine, but in everyday conversation, others sometimes strain to listen. This has affected my speeches too.

Believe me, I can project my voice if the situation warrants. Using air in my lungs, I push the words out of my mouth at a higher volume. I prefer not to yell, as the extra exertion sometimes makes me cough—plus yelling is unpleasant and generally not necessary.

Early on in my forensics competition days, I would inevitably lose my voice for no apparent reason. In high school, laryngitis would strike me, but there was no clear medical reason for it to occur. En route to competitions, my teammates and coach understood that I was not allowed to talk. My remedy, which worked amazingly well, was large mugs of warm water and lemons—lots of lemons. This remedy would give me just enough voice to compete and then it was back to voice rest.

In college, the laryngitis hit me harder. Between collegiate competitions and coaching forensics at a local high school, I was using my voice in many ways—from newsworthy speeches to dramatic interpretations. My voice was simply shot. At one point, in the most unmedical of terms, I was told that I had "split my vocal cords."

The NIDCD informs that vocal folds are two bands of muscle positioned across from each other in the larynx, which is between the tongue and trachea, one's airway.[vii] When one speaks, the vocal folds come together instantly as air from the lungs blows through them. The resulting vibration produces sound waves that become our spoken voice.

When I was told that my vocal cords were split, it actually meant that my vocal folds were stressed and not coming together naturally. I was sent to a speech pathologist for an assessment, and was diagnosed with functional dysphonia. It's a fancy way of saying that there was no obvious problem—not anatomical, neurological or psychological—that was affecting my vocal folds or larynx. Voice rest, and the warm water and lemons, were the cure for my lack of voice.

Eventually, when I stopped competing, the problem subsided. While I lose my voice far less often now, there are still occasional times that I struggle with extended periods of laryngitis. I usually know when a bout will hit me, like after an infrequent cold or fever, and then it's back to the water and lemons.

Pace Yourself

When delivering a speech or recitation, you need to speak at a normal pace. Yes, I know, what's normal? I can't answer that for you exactly, but I can tell you what to avoid.

Debate teams often learn to speak rapidly to pack in as many arguments as possible in the time allotted by the competition. Some of these folks speak fast, lightning fast!

They're not the only ones. Consider how dizzying it is to keep up with a professional auctioneer. You might hear in the period of half a minute, "Eighty-five, do I hear eighty-five? Eighty-five over in the blue shirt; Do I hear ninety, ninety— ninety to the gentleman in the red cap; Ninety-five? Who do I have for ninety-five? Ninety-five in the corner; One hundred? Do I hear one hundred? Going once, going twice . . . sold for ninety-five to the lady in the corner."

US Senator Conrad Burns was also a professional livestock auctioneer who volunteered to emcee charity auctions. When addressing the audience, he spoke at a conversational pace. Yet once the auction portion of the evening began, hold on to your seats! The talk was fast.

Aaron Sorkin's political drama, *The West Wing*, which aired from 1999-2006, provided a glimpse into the lives of fictional White House officials and advisors. The insiders were portrayed as speaking with each other at a frantic clip. Having worked on Capitol Hill, I can tell you that depiction is highly accurate! If you go back to watch the episodes, notice how the repartee among staffers was often swift, but exchanges with the public were less hurried.

As in the political realm, two people with the same core knowledge will speak more rapidly than if a less-knowing individual is involved. It might take you ten minutes to describe to a roofing professional where you found a leak in your home and how you think it occurred. Talking among themselves, these professionals may weigh your assessment and offer their own in a fraction of the time.

There are moments when a speaker, no matter how well-intentioned, may deliver words too slowly. A former federal judge testifying before a US House select committee, cognizant that his words would be captured before the august body, gave such gradual, measured responses that some public viewers expressed concern that he may have suffered a medical emergency. The judge acknowledged his intentionally slow pace, and assured on-lookers that he was perfectly healthy.

There is a sweet spot between being a fast-talker and a sleep walker. That spot is generally in the range of 120-150 spoken words per minute. To measure your particular speed, time yourself delivering part of your speech. Count the number of words in that section and divide by the number of minutes you took to present. This is your general speaking rate.

To help you gauge your own talks, I'll share that at a recent board presentation I purposefully spoke slowly in parts in order to add emphasis and clarity to my arguments. My rate for that speech was 146 words per minute. My usual rate is likely between 150 and 170 words per minute.

If you, or your audience, think you speak too fast or too slow, make adjustments. If you are a debater, try other forms of speaking (in addition to debate!) to help taper the speed. The same advice is true if you recite melancholy poetry, which tends to flow more leisurely. Try another form of speaking to increase your conversational speed.

The type of audience you are addressing will also figure into your pace. If you are addressing an audience where English is a second language, you might slow down so you are better understood. The same is true for highly technical presentations where new ideas must be grasped. Yet if you're running close to your time limit, you may want to pick up the pace to make all your points.

An unusual tip for adjusting your pace involves music. While practicing, play melodies softly from a device in the background. If you are trying to slow down, play Chopin, Liszt or restful concertos from other classical composers. To encourage a faster speaking rate, play a melody with a faster tempo like "Sabre Dance" by Khachaturian or "William Tell Overture" by Rossini.

Sometimes you will want to adjust your pace to match the intensity or tone of your speech. That's perfectly fine. In fact, it will keep the audience better engaged.

Chapter Three

Boost Your
Self-Esteem

Summon the Courage

Have you heard an internal voice telling you that what you have to say isn't important? You're not alone. Some people talk themselves into believing their thoughts aren't worthy of an audience. Or perhaps you feel that what you have to say is boring. You may be right, but it may be a chance you have to take.

Professionally, I often work with government officials, corporate leaders, and association executives. Once, while working with a coalition of organizations, I was summoned to the White House to discuss a health policy issue with senior administration advisors. Our coalition was composed of about ten people and, truth be told, we weren't exactly certain of the agenda for the meeting. But when the White House calls, it's best to answer.

After arriving at the White House, we were ushered into a stately conference room, and a number of officials, most of whom you've seen on television, took seats with us around the table. We were briefed on the administration's strategy on a particular policy matter, and then we were asked if there were questions or any other related issues to raise.

Silence.

My colleagues and I glanced apprehensively at each other. It was clear to us that this was not a meeting for open conversation. Nevertheless, there was a related matter of significant importance to the organization I represented that had been overlooked. I broke the silence, briefly explained the issue, and asked that it be considered. A couple of administration officials appeared to snicker and, while the taunt may not have been directed at me, I figured this was the last time I'd receive a White House invitation.

The meeting adjourned and my group was left to saunter out of the conference room and down the marble hallways. I'll never forget a colleague, Kathleen Teixeira, whispered to me, "Great job. I'm really glad you brought that up." Her words made all the difference in a trying situation, and it confirmed that speaking up is important when you have something to say.

I've been honored to be invited back to the White House.

When considering the pros and cons of speaking up, put the situation into context. My parents would sometimes say to me, "What's the worst that could happen?" I use that phrase frequently to weigh various actions.

In the White House example, if I didn't say anything, then the issue may never have been considered. If I spoke up and the issue was dismissed, then I might learn why and understand the reason for the lack of support. If I spoke up, and there was acknowledgement of the issue, then I would know there were allies for the policy. Unfortunately, sometimes your internal voice speaks loudly in your ear: If I speak up and no one likes what I say, will I be fired? Will I be kicked out of the coalition? Will people think I'm stupid?

The answer to these questions is, "Highly unlikely." If you've done your homework enough to understand the subject matter, and you respectfully address it, by all means speak up. You won't be fired or kicked out of the group, since you are actually doing your job. Who cares if someone thinks you're stupid? Prove them wrong by contributing well-researched information.

It may seem awkward at first, but the more you speak publicly, the more you will begin to counterprogram your internal negative voice.

With the White House situation, I accomplished my goal of raising an important issue in a challenging environment. My colleague's kind words helped to counter any doubts I may have had.

I'm far from the only person to raise questions in a professional setting. Julie Cantor Weinberg is a government affairs executive in Washington, DC, who has represented high-profile organizations. I don't believe I have ever been in a meeting with Julie in which she hasn't asked a question of a speaker. Usually, her questions aim to clarify a policy point, but sometimes they appear to draw attention to an issue of importance to her employer. Regardless, Julie's line of questioning is not frivolous. She exudes confidence when raising her hand. She clearly thinks about what she is going to say and the impact it may have.

To boost your self-esteem when speaking publicly, remember that something you say may assist someone else. You are imparting wisdom, or entertainment, or information.

I understand there may still be this internal voice telling you your words aren't good enough. There are ways to counter that nag. For one, stop watching TED Talks. Now let me say up front that I admire greatly what TED has accomplished in bringing ideas and the spoken word to millions. I have attended a TEDx Conference and was inspired and energized at the conclusion of it. Several friends have presented at these conferences and I admire greatly the grit and tenacity that they put into their talks. I like to watch TED Talks. However, if you're trying to boost your self-esteem, stop watching them for a while.

Most people do not speak as though they are delivering a well-rehearsed TED Talk. If you're trying to feel better about your own speaking abilities, listen to talks that aren't quite as polished.

A friend of mine, Portia Clark, is a civic leader who I had encouraged to run for office. After sitting together one weekend during a marathon county board meeting where one could listen to officials speak incessantly on trifling matters, Portia whispered, "Why would I want to spend my time listening to this?" We laughed quietly from the back of the room.

She had a point, but let's look at this as a learning moment. We were watching several examples of how not to speak publicly. One person had difficulty putting words into a cogent sentence; another did not think critically about the matter at hand; and more than one felt the need to pontificate on points already raised by other colleagues. All are actions we should strive to avoid.

This is not a "mean girls" drill. Remember, nobody is perfect, and it's not polite to criticize people who are trying or are just being human. Instead, watch those speeches that have human flaws. Watch commencement addresses given by the less-than-famous, listen to speeches from the not-quite-ready-for-TED individuals, and chances are you'll learn something. It should make you feel better about your own entrée into public speaking.

I find it inspiring to listen to people take a brave step into public speaking, no matter their shortcomings. There was a highly engaged volunteer in our state who decided to run for public office among a crowded slate of candidates. Whether you agreed with his positions or not, he was by far the best versed in policy matters and knew the minutiae of most local issues. There was no one on the dais who had more experience or depth of knowledge than him. Yet he was an awful public speaker. His tone was somewhat arrogant, his arms flailed, his mannerisms were off-putting. He did not win, yet he listened to his well-meaning critics and received coaching to improve his skills. He ran again and appeared a much more competent candidate.

Surround yourself with some well-meaning supporters. These should be people who want to help you improve and are not hesitant to offer constructive advice. You don't have to adopt all their recommendations, but you should realize some improvements in your presentations that will boost your confidence moving forward.

Sometimes the best boost for your self-confidence is to just get up and try. Mickey Trimarchi, a former journalist, decided to try his hand at something he had never done before: acting. He auditioned for a role in a repertory theater play and, to his surprise, was cast among the leads. With personal practice and formal rehearsals, Mickey went on to deliver a performance worthy of the sustained applause he received.

A neighbor of mine had never risen to speak on an issue before an elected body. She felt strongly about an issue with a local park, so she decided it was time to express publicly her frustration with the matter. Not only was she heard, but the *Sun Gazette* quoted part of her statement. Her voice made a difference.

Now, you might not meet the famous playwright, Emmy award–winning Ken Levine, like Mickey did, or be quoted in the paper, like my neighbor was, but sometimes just the thrill of trying is all the boost you need to keep speaking up.

Once you do give a speech or compete in a forensics competition, take a moment to acknowledge what you've accomplished. Whether it's a goofy TikTok dance with your best buds, a pizza dinner, or a giant hug from someone close to you, do something to reward yourself. It will make you feel good and boost your confidence for the next time you get up to speak.

As you eat that pizza or high five your colleague, remember, too, to appreciate the feedback you receive along the way. Someone might say, "I liked your tie," after your talk. It may not seem like much of a compliment, but it tells you that your appearance was on the mark. Someone else might say that they agreed with your points, they liked the story you told, or they thought you had a nice smile. These praises—both small and big—help you know you're on the right track and boost your confidence. Be sure to thank the person who offered the kind word (and maybe they'll do it again!).

Practice Makes Better

My brother has a strong reputation as a national sales director. He's great at managing people and delivering sales assessments to his company. His work requires speaking publicly. When he was getting started in the industry, he would call his sister (that would be me) to practice his talks. Over the phone, I would insist he repeat phrases until they were smooth and became second nature for him. Because we're siblings, there were no holds barred when it came to critiques. Thanks to the effort he made, his speeches were well received by his managers and colleagues.

When I have to deliver certain public pronouncements, I usually phone a friend too. It helps to speak aloud the words in my head to see if they resonate properly with an audience— even a practice audience of one. Remember, even the esteemed Rep. John Lewis practiced before his family's chickens!

After a talk, taking informal critique from the audience will help prepare you better for the next one. If you're at a conference or public event, most people only want to be polite.

They'll say, "I enjoyed your talk," or, "Thanks for coming." All of which is very nice to hear. You might try thanking the person for their kindness and then inquiring about what they liked most and least about your presentation. Sometimes you'll pick up helpful tips. After one such exchange, one lady said she liked my talk but that the content was a little simple and obvious. Through all the accolades that day, it was the best piece of feedback I received, and it helped me to elevate my content.

Certain types of speaking may be outside of your general comfort zone. You may be great at delivering the sales talk, but reciting poetry is not your thing. Or reciting a story is something you enjoy doing, but speaking extemporaneously on a public policy matter is definitely not. All the more reason to give these unfamiliar fields a try.

When I was coaching, more than a couple of students were hardcore debaters. They most defiantly never wanted to try extemporaneous or prose. With some persuading (okay, a lot of persuading), they competed in these other categories. They won tournaments. Some even begrudgingly liked the new genres. By practicing these different styles, they improved their speaking skills overall. Some found that their debate prowess was enriched as a result.

For the sheer heck of it, I competed collegiately as a pentathlete. Extemporaneous speaking was my thing, but I was comfortable with other policy types of speech. Performing a dramatic interpretation was outside of my comfort zone, but I did it anyway. No one will nominate me for an Academy Award. Frankly, dramatic interpretation competitions are not about acting and are not considered theater craft. Instead, dramatic interpretation lets the speaker recite excerpts from a published dramatic play, novel, or short story within a specified time range. Some people will read their excerpt in one voice, while others may choose to portray different characters by changing their pitch, tone, or accent.

Voicing dramatic elements can help with other types of speaking roles. Dramatic interpretation will help you learn about the flow of a speech, the expressiveness of your words, and ways to polish your gestures and poise.

Practicing aloud gives you the opportunity to focus on your speech. This may seem obvious, but hear me out. When I practice, I find myself over-embellishing areas of the speech. I want to be natural in my delivery, so I keep talking to explain a point. Inevitably, it's just too much talking! A point that might take two minutes to explain becomes a ten-minute explanation during my practice round. I drag my speech down with these supposed enhancements, and I likely wouldn't notice it if I didn't voice the speech beforehand.

Many people fall into this trap. At a technical conference, a knowledgeable speaker on testing accuracy presented information on a precarious new industry. The data presented was stunning and made a strong argument for industry oversight. However, the speaker repeated the information so often that its initial impact was somewhat lost. By practicing aloud in advance, the speaker would have heard the duplication and may have adjusted to make a more powerful presentation.

As you practice, think about what your audience might glean from your talk. Do you want them to learn something new, advocate for a position, or merely enjoy your words? Are there elements that are extraneous to your talk? If so, remove them. Are you having trouble clearly expressing a point? If so, keep saying it over and over again until you have it down pat and it sounds smooth.

An elected official was practicing a short speech with me. He had all the latest buzz words inserted into his talk. While he felt that he was covering the political landscape, I couldn't understand a word he said. In truth, I don't think he understood a word he said, either. As he practiced aloud in front of me, he started to realize that his words were meaningless. He was able to *hear* his speech, not just read it, and thus made positive changes.

Reality television singing shows often have judges who tell contestants to "make a song their own." The same is true when you practice. If you read prose or poetry aloud, it will sound different than when you read it in your brain. Listen for where you pause and which words you emphasize. Sometimes, you will need to speak a passage repeatedly until you achieve the proper cadence and connotation.

A fun way to practice is to take the lyrics of your favorite song, just like those reality shows, and speak them aloud. While it's tempting, don't sing the words. Speak the lyrics and test your pronunciation, pausing, and breathing.

When identifying songs to use, look for ones with variety. A song that merely says "yeah, yeah, yeah" or "oh baby" might have a swell tune, but might not live up to a practice challenge. There are millions of songs to consider, but here are a few to get you thinking: "What About Us?" (by Alecia B. Moore, John McDaid, Steve Mac); "Superstition" (by Stevie Wonder); "Windmills of Your Mind" (by Michel Legrand, Alan Bergman, Marilyn Bergman); "The Sound of Music" (by Richard Rodgers and Oscar Hammerstein); "Children Will Listen" (by Stephen Sondheim); and "The Earth Song" (by Michael Jackson).

Do you find the same meaning in speaking the words as you do when you listen to the song as it's sung, or are you capturing it in a new way? When the tune is absent, are you expressing the words differently than in the melodic version? You may find new significance to the spoken words.

When you go back to your speech, consider recording it. Set up a video to capture your talk and movements. You might record just sections of the speech at first. Afterward, play it back to assess the positive aspects and identify areas you wish to improve. Eventually, you may record from start to finish. This will allow you to clock your presentation to make sure you stay within the allotted time. You can always delete these practice rounds when you're through.

Know Your Audience

It's easy to get wrapped up in your speech and all the preparation for it. You think it's all about you, what you plan to say, and how you will deliver those words. But really, it's not about you. It's about the audience.

Is the audience understanding what you're saying? Are they laughing or crying or cheering in all the right places? Are they bored or are they engaged? What are they thinking?

A former boyfriend was none too pleased that I liked to ask him, "What are you thinking?" "Nothing!" was often the response (and it's probably why the word "former" applies here). Yet it's a technique to use in certain public speaking situations. If I'm giving a technical presentation, I might stop at one point and ask the audience, "Does this make sense?" and then wait for nods or quizzical looks. (Do not do this as often as I did with that boyfriend; it's a turn-off.)

Aside from direct questioning, there are other ways to know if you're making a connection. When you accept an invitation to speak, ask the host what information people most want to glean from your presentation. It will help you focus your remarks. I've also mentioned that it's helpful to make acquaintances in advance of your talk. These connections will help you gauge the mood of the room.

It takes some practice, but there are ways for you to read your audience. One is simply to observe people. Is the audience paying attention? Are all eyes on the speaker? If so, you're on the right track.

Inevitably, some people will yawn, some may rudely chat with others, and some may be engrossed in their phones. Remember, these behaviors may have nothing to do with you. The person yawning may have been up half the night with a colicky baby. The person talking may be asking someone for an extra pen. The person on their phone may have a work-related emergency to address. You may be a stellar speaker, but people will be human in their behavior.

That said, watch the audience for clues on what adjustments you are able to make. I used to lecture at a university where the class was three hours long. I bore myself listening to me talk for that length of time, never mind the students! So I adjusted the class to include discussion sessions and guest speakers. It seemed to keep the students (and me) better engaged.

If you're reciting poetry or a selection from a novel and you feel the audience's attention waning, try to adjust the tone or volume of your presentation to bring them back around. If someone is rudely interrupting your speech with a loud sidebar conversation, you might stop speaking, smile, and wait for the individuals to stop. Usually, other audience members will help to quiet the disturbance so you may begin speaking again.

Depending on the nature of your talk, you may also reengage people by asking the audience specific questions. For a speech on cybersecurity, ask for a show of hands to see how many people changed their passwords this week. A talk on pets might be enhanced with a poll on the number of cat, dog, and turtle owners.

If there is a period for questions and answers after your talk, you'll have the opportunity to understand more directly what's on the mind of your audience. Be sure to thank each individual for their questions and answer them to the best of your ability. If you do not know the answer, it's okay to say so. You might offer to follow up with a response at a later time.

If you are asked your opinion on a matter but have not picked a side, it's perfectly fine to admit it. Listeners often appreciate a direct, honest response. For example, let's say your speech is about the history of unions. After your talk, a spectator asks you if the local coffee shop should unionize. If you're unsure of your position on the matter, you might offer a response like, "As you may gather from my speech, I am a strong proponent of the unions organized in the early 1900s, but I am still undecided about the necessity of unions today. It is not clear to me that the benefits outweigh the costs, but I am open to learning more." You might also consider asking the audience member for more information: "Are you an employee of the coffee shop? What do you think?"

You may have the misfortune to experience a heckler. This is actually a rather rare occurrence, so don't sweat it. In case it happens to you, there are a variety of ways to respond. You might laugh and offer a clever retort (although this usually won't stop someone who is headstrong about interrupting). You might try addressing the person directly: "Thanks for your advice." Sometimes it's easier to just take a moment to listen to the heckler, and then continue on with your talk. You might also stop speaking until the intruding voice is removed from the room.

The most important tip for handling a heckler is to keep yourself calm and collected. Remember, it's not about you; it's about someone who is feeling aggrieved or wants attention. The heckler might hurl personal insults to try to get a reaction from you. Don't take the bait. Don't insult the person back. You are the speaker and you have credibility. Don't let a rude troublemaker try to knock you down.

The truth is, a heckler can be unnerving. I experienced one during a presentation I was giving to community leaders. Someone in the audience was upset—not at my talk, but about a related subject. He was passionate about the matter and raised his voice while I was speaking. At first, I tried to speak louder, hoping it would drown him out. That was futile. Then I turned to him and said I understood his concern, but that I was discussing something else. He continued to shout. I asked him to allow me to finish my talk and offered to meet with him afterward. Someone in the audience came up beside him and quietly tried to calm him down. Eventually, the matter subsided and I continued my talk. The whole exchange lasted about a minute, but it was memorable to me because it was unexpected. I doubt anyone else in the audience gave it another thought.

All in all, while you are working to present your best self, remember that you have the power to manage the audience too. Look for the signs and adjust accordingly.

Chapter Four

What to Say

Why Are You Speaking?

"For what reason does the gentlelady rise?" is a phrase you'll hear on the floor of the US House of Representatives, the US Senate, and statehouses across the country. It is used by the Speaker or Chair to ask why a legislator wishes to speak. Likely no one will ask you why you "rise" before you open your mouth to speak, but you should know the purpose of your talk.

Think about what you want to say. Do you want to inform your audience, inspire them, or persuade them? What is your message? What does your audience need to hear from you? These questions need answers, no matter the type of speech you plan to deliver. With an extemporaneous speech or an original oratory, or merely speaking up in class or meetings, you should consider the impact of your words.

A nonprofit organization asked me to give an address to its members during an annual meeting. There were a few hundred people in the room who wanted to hear an update on the many activities of this highly engaged organization. While there were no limitations placed on my talk, I needed to assess *why* I was speaking. As a member of the board of directors, my role was to help hire the chief executive officer. Board members also assess and set a direction and strategy for the organization. For me to reach the podium to discuss new programming or financial targets would have been inappropriate. It's not *why* I was to speak. There were other people—from the CEO to the vice presidents—who would provide operational details. Instead, I focused on why someone would want to hear from a board member. I welcomed members for attending and applauded their work during a turbulent time; I explained that the board clarified the organization's by-laws and created a code of ethics; and I closed by congratulating the CEO and his team for their work, which would be detailed later. *Why* I was speaking was made clear.

Listen intently to the speeches of others to determine why they are speaking. Musical superstar Beyoncé has created an enormous platform for her art and ideas. Beyoncé expresses herself through her music and dance. She is photographed frequently as a fashion icon and model. Yet have you noticed that she rarely says a word? When she does speak, millions—from her Beyhive fans to readers of popular magazines and social media—listen. She appears to give great thought to *why* she raises her voice.

Of course, we don't all have platforms that match the magnitude of Beyoncé's. To be heard, we must carefully consider the purpose of raising our voices.

A public comment period precedes most meetings of a local county board. Citizens who file a speaker's slip are given two to five minutes to address a community issue. Speakers are called, one at a time, to a microphone in the front of the room to address the board members. The variety of topics can range from informative to compelling and, at times, entertaining. People discuss stormwater management, sports field data analytics, flying gondolas, racial equity, and management of electric scooters, among many other subjects.

The more effective speakers can tell you why they are speaking. They usually know their issue is coming before the board for deliberation, and they want to be able to influence the outcome. Or they believe the county has not listened sufficiently to evidence and they want to express their views in a public forum. Or they intend to inform the board of a matter that is not yet common knowledge. Some speakers rise to show solidarity with a particular action, thereby giving the board support for an imminent vote.

On the federal level, individuals may be asked to testify before a congressional committee or a federal commission. There, too, the more effective speakers will be able to tell you why they have been invited or why they are compelled to address the panel. Some people speak to draw attention to an issue or to provide greater detail on a matter to the policymakers.

Some people prefer not to draw attention to a matter, so they construct their comments in a way that tries to deflect from a situation. If a company's chief executive is asked to speak about the high prices charged for its products, the executive might only discuss the quality and public value of its merchandise in order to avoid raising flags about the prices. No matter the speaking strategy, it is all part of the purpose in speaking.

My professional work encompasses strategic and business development for a wide variety of health and science issues. A major piece of legislation, which held great significance for some of the matters I advise, would revamp the food safety system as overseen by the Food and Drug Administration (FDA). It was signed into law in 2011.

Provisions of the law, the Food Safety Modernization Act, addressed produce standards, hazard analysis, foreign supplier verification, sanitary transportation of food, and more. There was one section of this comprehensive law that focused on model laboratory standards for food testing. It was noteworthy because at that point US laboratories that tested food for pathogens and other contaminants were under no obligation to follow quality standards. The law would attempt to remedy this oversight.

After passage of the law, FDA hearings were held to gather public input on how to implement it. Despite its importance, little was said initially about the food testing provision. My role was to bring this matter to the forefront. After successfully raising awareness of the issue, not a hearing occurred without someone rising to speak on the value of laboratory standards and the quality of food testing. This raising of voices on a defined purpose led to FDA regulation on food testing.

Congressional briefings provide another outlet for speakers to express themselves for a defined purpose. The Alliance for Health Policy, a nonpartisan organization seeking to educate on complex health policy matters, hosts lunch events featuring various experts. With four or five experts seated on each event panel, these individuals speak to a specific topic, like "comparative effectiveness research" or "models for better care at lower cost" or "emerging issues with biosimilars." They each expound on their areas of policy and research expertise. They aren't necessarily all great orators. The way some of these arcane subjects are presented is sleep-inducing if you're not a policy wonk. Yet all these speakers share an important point: They unite in their purpose for speaking.

I like listening to authors who speak at events touting their latest books. From children's books by Madelyn Rosenberg to thoughts on artificial intelligence by Ray Kurzweil to books about vegetarianism and farming by Jonathan Safran Foer, these authors inform and inspire. Of course, authors would like for you to buy their books, but there is much that may be learned by listening to them speak. Their overall purpose is to share their knowledge, ideas, thought processes, and stories.

Likewise, members of the clergy in their weekly or holiday sermons often offer insight on human conduct or issues of the day. They may aim for their congregations to learn empathy, reflect on their behavior, or become more charitable. Some wish to expound on a portion of sacred text. After holidays, some gather to compare what was learned from various religious talks. The better sermons infuse humor, personal experiences, and a strong message.

A good friend of mine decided to switch careers and became an ordained minister. He is a natural speaker, very folksy and relatable, but he was apprehensive about his first sermons to his congregants. I agreed to serve as a sounding board for him. Late on weeknights, we would sneak into the church. He would present his sermon from the pulpit and I would critique it from the pews. He was able to hone his messaging to deliver a talk with a clear purpose. We vowed never to reveal to his congregants that a Jewish girl helped him craft a Christian sermon. We figured if Jewish composers were responsible for "White Christmas," "Rudolph the Red-Nosed Reindeer," and "Santa Baby," his church could survive my liturgical tweaks.

Lectures held by local professional groups are ubiquitous speech occasions. Usually held over a dinner or lunch, these events feature speakers who address specific issues. The Rotary Club might ask one of its members to discuss international travel, and the area gardening society might host a lecture on how to cull invasive plants. The local chamber of commerce might ask a keynote speaker to explain how they grew their business. The AARP chapter may host talks on financial planning, and the local medical society may ask a physician to present on an interesting case.

Each of these groups has their own flavor and preferences for presentations. After sitting through dozens of surgical lectures, over dinner no less, I never cringe at the sight of a slide show filled with blood, organs, and intestines. In fact, it nearly made me consider becoming a surgeon (if I could have skipped the years of med school and residency). Yet there are many people who could not stomach such presentations. They are not the target audience for these talks.

A few years ago, I published a book of photographs called *As We Are*, which intended to reveal a historically Black community in its current state. Images taken at public events and from neighborhood wanderings highlighted the community's beauty and strength before a planned period of revitalization began. The photographs also exposed troubling and entrenched barriers.

After publication, I was asked to speak about the book at various functions ranging from a gallery show to a church luncheon to a seniors' social group. At each engagement I had a different reason for speaking.

There were many familiar faces at the gallery show, including people whose photos were featured in the book. My intention at this gathering was to inspire the audience. The book explained how the tight-knit community was joyful and engaged but still struggled with physical and social barriers. My message pointed this out and encouraged all to work in unison to tear down remaining obstacles.

At the church luncheon, my aim was to inform the audience of aspects of their broader community that they may not have seen previously. Some were surprised to learn that razor wire still lined a public trail and that a segregation wall continued to stand in this part of the county. It was an informational session with some audience members asking questions about historical elements of the area.

At the seniors' group, I hoped to convey that this historically Black community continued to wrestle with matters that others take for granted. I wanted the audience to leave with something to discuss with their friends and neighbors, and to realize that they, too, should speak out if the opportunity arises.

There are people who speak merely to hear the sound of their voice. There's an adage that says, "The wise speak because they have something to say. Fools speak because they have to say something." Plenty of people speak for attention. Sure, it's a "purpose," but it's not necessarily an effective one. If you haven't identified a purpose in speaking, it may be best to remain silent.

I was asked to address a regional medical association about how government actions would affect their particular specialty. It was a full-day conference and I was among the last speakers. All the preceding talks presented highly technical, clinical data to a packed auditorium. By the time my speech came along, the room was pretty well cleared out. It's a little unnerving when that happens, but I didn't take it personally since I hadn't yet spoken a word. That said, while I had relevant information to share, the purpose of my speech may not have aligned well with the membership's main interests.

Reciting prose or poetry, another form of public speaking, may be for the purpose of mere enjoyment or to share appreciation of a literary work. When selecting such a recitation, consider what the piece means to you. Does it tell a story of personal significance? Do you admire the writing style of the author? Does the tone or scheme match your speaking style? Do you wish to impart knowledge from the literary piece?

Think about how much time is allotted for your recitation. During that limited time, what do you want to express to the audience? You may want them to understand the totality of the author's work, or you may only have an interest in a particular segment of the piece.

Let me illustrate this with an extreme example. No one is likely to listen to you recite the 1,200-plus pages of Leo

Tolstoy's *War and Peace*. However, you could splice together excerpts to help the audience understand, in about five to seven minutes, how the work chronicles the lives of Russian aristocratic families during the Napoleonic era or how it explains the coexistence of war and peace. Or you might instead use your time to portray the struggles and passions of one of the family members. In making these decisions, you might consider your personal affinity for the literary piece as well as your approach to speaking the words.

A high school teammate adored reciting "The Love Song of J. Alfred Prufrock" by T. S. Eliot, a modernist poem exploring refrains of indecision, inadequacy, and relationships. I never quite understood why, but every time she spoke the opening words, "Let us go then, you and I / When the evening is spread out against the sky," this American teenager adopted a British accent she had never used before. To her, the words called for this new voice. The poem brought out that meaning for her.

You might hear speakers present other types of affectations. Some people will mimic a southern accent, even though they've never stepped foot outside of Maine. I've heard policy-makers, who only speak English, use a strong Spanish accent for certain words. Vocal fry, or lowering one's vocal register to the point that it crackles, is a trend among some reality show celebrities. You should consider if these mannerisms, whether consciously adopted or not, actually enhance your recitation or if they seem fake.

A library of works is available to select a theme and tone that suits you. Elizabeth Barrett Browning wrote "The Cry of the Children," a poem that speaks of child labor, and *Sonnets from the Portuguese*, a book noted for its expression of fervent love. Rudyard Kipling, in his book *Rewards and Fairies*, wrote the poem, "If—" to pass on wisdom about how to live life. Countée Cullen and Langston Hughes, poets who shaped the Harlem Renaissance, wrote collections in disparate styles about race, dreams, and America. This is a mere sampling of the literary works available for recitation.

Whether you are speaking on a topic of your choosing or someone has assigned a subject to you, find words that reflect what you want to express. Your purpose should be clear.

How the audience perceives your words is another matter. You may present an informational talk that actually inspires someone to change their mind on the subject. You may try to persuade someone of your position but end up entrenching the audience further into their own views. You may recite a poem that helps someone view the world in a new light.

While you can't control what others think, you can focus your remarks and be clear. All speakers should have a purpose.

Speaking (Forensics) Genres

Public speaking assumes a variety of forms. Certainly, length is one determinant. You might speak impromptu for five minutes or present a one-hour oration, or something in between. While you might have free rein to speak as long as you desire, chances are there is some limitation. A class or conference event will have tight schedules to follow. A forensics competition has time limits in each category of speech. Even if the clock is not ticking officially, there are limits to the audience's attention span.

Think about the type of speech you want to give. You might deliver a written speech, lob off-the-cuff remarks on a given topic, or recite an imagined story. For speech and debate competitions on the academic level, there are a range of categories from which to choose. You might enjoy reciting prose from a favorite novel, or, if you like to make people laugh, a humorous interpretation may be your style. Poetry slams and storytelling showcase an individual's creativity. Giving an extemporaneous speech on current issues related to domestic or international affairs can be a challenge to attempt. Delivering a societal or political commentary may be something to try as well.

There are many styles of debate from which to choose. You might select Lincoln-Douglas debate, where two individuals go toe-to-toe on questions of societal values. This style is influenced by Abraham Lincoln and Stephen Douglas who, in 1858, considered societal questions on the prohibition of slavery. More current Lincoln-Douglas debate might address topics like guaranteed universal income, restorative justice, and firearms bans.

There are also policy debates, once referred to as four-man debate, where two-person teams face each other to present a case for or against a predetermined resolution. Examples might range from "The United States government should require vaccination of its citizens against pandemic viral diseases" to "The president of the United States should be elected directly by the people" to "The United States government should prioritize cybersecurity over data privacy."

Other debate formats simulate governmental bodies like the US Congress or the United Nations. Some organizations offer mock trials that replicate a courtroom and give participants a chance to argue a legal case.

In high school, I was appointed to Girls State, a national competitive program run in all fifty states by the American Legion Auxiliary. At Girls State, you join young women from your state in creating a mock government. Upon arrival to this week-long camp, participants are assigned a political party (either Federalist or Nationalist) and a fake city in which to live. If I remember correctly, we wore beanies to depict our assigned party—mine was blue. As you are tasked with setting up your city government, and then an overall state structure, there is a lot of debating and speech-making taking place. Girls from all over the state competed to become "mayor" of their city and debated policy issues that would inform their city's charter.

On the mock state level, candidates for governor, lieutenant governor, and attorney general emerged, and the debates continued. For an inside glimpse, there is a fantastic documentary called *Boys State* by Jesse Moss and Amanda McBaine that won the 2020 Sundance Film Festival US Grand Jury Prize.

I did not run for mayor or governor, but I was intrigued with another offering: Girls Nation. Each mock city would select a candidate for the US Senate. These candidates would appear before the entire Girls State to deliver a platform speech on why they should be selected to represent their state on the national level. I was selected as my city's representative and basically had the midnight hours to develop a speech to deliver to over six hundred people in the morning. The body then voted for two senators and I was one of them. Weeks later I was in Washington, DC, replicating the Girls State experience, but with ninety-nine other girls from across the country drafting bills, creating resolutions, and running for national office. The experience was exhilarating and demonstrates the power of speech and debate.

You may be invited to give a keynote address at a national conference or make formal remarks as part of a panel of experts. Your company may ask you to explain to management a professional project for which you are responsible. Maybe you feel passionate about a school board issue and want to speak up during a public comment period. Or someone wants you to present to a seniors' group at a local community center about your recent travels or read your poetry aloud at a heritage festival. The forms of speaking are endless.

There are formal categories of speaking that are often used on the collegiate level. A few of them are explored below: original oratory, extemporaneous, impromptu, and readings and interpretations. While these are official competition categories, the speaking styles are universal.

Original Oratory

For competitive speaking, original oratory applies rules from national bodies, such as the National Speech and Debate Association, or has rules set by local organizations like chapters of AAUW (American Association of University Women), Future Farmers of America, or Rotary Club. An original oratory must be, well, original—not a paraphrased version of someone else's talk. Speeches in this category emphasize persuasion and memorization. Generally, original oratories last no longer than ten minutes.

Outside of competition, there are many opportunities to give a speech that you wrote. Whether at a scientific conference, a charity dinner, or a PTA meeting where you're pleading for school funding, the skill sets are similar. The time limitations differ and the speech might be informational, inspirational, or just plain entertaining.

So what oration will you give?

If a teacher assigns you a speech on the lasting impact of William Shakespeare and you have no interest in Shakespeare, it's likely that your presentation will be lackluster. It's your responsibility as the speaker to make your oration worth a listen. Try refining the assignment and making it your own.

How do you prove the premise that Shakespeare's influence is lasting without being boring? If you have an interest in music, pointing out Shakespeare's enduring relevance in this area may make the subject matter more appealing to you *and* the audience. Just look at all the examples from which to draw material. The 1970s song "Cruel to be Kind" by Nick Lowe and Ian Gomm came from *Hamlet*'s Prince who said to his mother, "I must be cruel only to be kind." The title of Mumford & Sons' album *Sigh No More* is a phrase from *Much Ado About Nothing*. Rocker Lou Reed wrote "Romeo Had Juliette," a song about two lovers torn apart by their New York families. The band Radiohead wrote "Exit Music (For a Film)" as the closing song to the Baz Luhrmann movie *Romeo + Juliet*, starring Leonardo DiCaprio and Claire Danes. The 1950s Cole Porter musical *Kiss Me Kate* is a musical rendition of *The Taming of the Shrew*. Details such as these will help to draw in the audience and persuade them of the premise.

You might even get extra points for singing a few lines during your oration.

One of the most effective orations I heard was from Dennis O'Leary, MD, then-president of the Joint Commission on Accreditation of Healthcare Organizations, during his presentation at the inaugural conference of the Institute for Quality in Laboratory Medicine. Dr. O'Leary was one of the many luminaries at the conference recognized for innovative contributions to improvements in laboratory medicine. Other health care superstars took the stage first. Each, with their PowerPoint presentations, had pearls of wisdom to impart on the willing audience of laboratory-related professionals. Dr. O'Leary then arrived without PowerPoint, without a teleprompter, without an abstract, without much of anything but his voice. He shared his views on the need for national quality goals and the importance of the "do no harm" principle in health care. All eyes were on him and the story he imparted. It was powerful.

It brings home the point that you should speak on a topic about which you are passionate or, at least, knowledgeable. Sometimes it's difficult to find that sweet spot. Some students, when asked what interests them, may simply answer "sports." All at once that gives you too much and too little to decipher. It's generally too broad a topic to hone in on a persuasive speech, and "sports" alone doesn't provide much detail.

Here's where you need to dig a little deeper. Ask yourself, "What type of sports?" Let's say the answer is football. Okay, what do you like about football? Is it the intricacies of the game? Understanding the rules? Or is it about team loyalty, tailgating, or favorite players?

One of my nephews is a fan of the New England Patriots. We really don't understand how that happened. He's never lived in Boston. In fact, I don't think he had even been to Boston when he found his favorite team. So what is it about the Patriots? Tom Brady. He admires the quarterback for his athletic abilities. (And no, I don't know if he switched allegiance to the Tampa Bay Buccaneers when Brady transferred.)

Getting back to original oratory, someone who only likes sports may now be positioned to give a speech on how leading quarterbacks influence team allegiances.

At times, you may find yourself so enthralled with an issue that you have too much to say. I often have this problem when giving a report or update on government affairs topics. I err on the side of giving too many details including how an issue evolved, the positions of the key stakeholders, the strategy behind various policy options, and—oh yeah—an update. I do this partially to make certain that everyone in the room is up to speed on the matter and that a good discussion is generated with the audience. I also over-reveal in these talks because it's fun and I hate to miss any detail.

That said, don't do it. A more effective oratory is concise and builds on targeted content.

Another way to look at this is to examine a contemporary issue in granular detail. Take the issue of climate change. This is a broad topic to cover in a ten-minute speech. If your main goal is less about climate change and more about how to change human behavior to support the planet, you have now narrowed your topic to something more palatable. Go even further: What steps do people need to take to affect change and why? What will the results be?

If your choice of oratory topics is unlimited, it can sometimes be just as challenging to find the right subject for you. To get you started, here are some topics to consider:

How to choose the perfect coffee shop

Should the United States be responsible for supplying vaccines to the world?

Should election voting be mandatory?

Do women apologize too much?

Are technology companies getting too big?

Should you wear white after Labor Day?

When should you dial 911?

Are we living in a civilized society?

What's the line between college athletics and professional sports?

How to make the perfect shakshuka

Should amusement parks be regulated for safety?

Socratic versus didactic: Which learning style is best?

Should the US build a high-speed rail network?

The new rules of dating

Is anything private anymore?

Is the world ready for the next pandemic?

How to make a million dollars

Opera, country, pop, reggaeton: How are musical genres related?

Is there a national mental health crisis?

The only real limitation on your topic is your imagination. Remember, you must have a purpose for speaking or, in this case, a point to your oration. If in competition, you may need to persuade the audience of your viewpoint. All orations should be informative.

Before you write your speech, map out its framework. One way to start is by creating a purpose box to capture what you want to say and how you want to say it. Here's an example:

PURPOSE BOX
Topic:
Purpose of the speech:
General points to support the topic:
Target audience:

Keep the purpose box nearby as you write your speech. It will help remind you of your focus and eliminate unnecessary components.

In general, think about your talk in three parts: introduction, main points, and conclusion.

The introduction should aim to grab the audience's attention, state the topic, and explain why it is important (or why you are discussing it). This may be accomplished in a matter-of-fact way, or you might weave in a story. Consider these examples in a speech entitled, "We still learn from Mister Rogers."

Example 1. Matter-of-fact

Mister Rogers' Neighborhood was an educational children's television series that ran for over thirty years on PBS. Its creator, Fred Rogers, would enter his home, put a red sweater on over his shirt and tie, and don a pair of sneakers in order to connect better with the children at home watching him on the screen. He asked children to be his neighbor and to join him in meeting new people, singing songs, and learning fresh ideas. He helped children understand their worries and encouraged them to accept themselves. These lessons are universal. Although Fred Rogers passed away many years ago, we still learn from Mister Rogers.

Example 2. Story

My cousin Ted grew up in a turbulent household. He had clothes to wear and enough to eat, but times were tough and his parents fought a lot. They eventually got a divorce. Ted was very young at the time, but he remembers being confused by the situation. With all the turbulence at home, Ted would try to escape by watching TV. *Mister Rogers' Neighborhood* was one of his favorite shows. Mister Rogers would put on his familiar red sweater and sneakers and then speak directly to Ted, asking him about his day. Together they would sing the song "Sometimes People are Good." Mister Rogers told Ted that people have lots of ways of feeling. Most importantly, Mister Rogers always told Ted that he was special. Ted struggled with his family situation throughout his childhood, but today he is a happy, successful elementary school teacher with two children of his own. From time to time, he hums Mister Rogers's songs to remind himself of the goodness inside him. After all these years, we still learn from Mister Rogers.

How you approach the introduction is up to you, but do remember to state upfront the reason for your talk.

The next section, the body of the speech, is where you should further explore your purpose and support it with examples, evidence, and details. You will want your audience to remember your main points, so keep them to a manageable number. Usually, three to five points are enough to make your case and stay within your time limitations.

Let's say the purpose of your speech is to argue that homework is an important component of schoolwork. After your introduction, you will need to outline the points supporting your premise. Your points might include:

Homework develops a student's self-discipline.

Homework improves a student's retention and understanding of material.

Homework helps a teacher gauge how well students are learning the material.

Consider each point as a separate paragraph where you expand on the meaning. So for the first point—homework develops a student's self-discipline—you might support the statement by providing a quote from a scholarly paper, explaining exactly how self-discipline is developed through homework, and supplying statistics on the success of self-disciplined students.

Remember, you are giving an oration to inform and persuade the audience. You are not writing a doctoral thesis. Provide enough evidence to support your point and then move on.

To move between points, it's fine to say, "number one," or "first," "second," and so forth. It also may help to add transition words like "next" or "then."

In the conclusion, summarize your main points and make a closing statement. The conclusion is also an opportunity to rebut outside arguments. Using the homework example, you might say, "Some of my peers argue that homework takes too much time, and I agree that the amount of homework given should be reasonable based on the age and grade level of the student. Yet the application of homework as a learning and growth tool is too important to eliminate."

Close on a memorable note. This may be with a story that links to your introduction, a personal anecdote, or a call to action. It may also be simply hammering home the reason for your talk.

This framework—introduction, main points, conclusion—works no matter the purpose of your oration. It's a great outline for getting started and will serve you well when you become more experienced, too. Remember, the outline need not be rigid. You may use it to weave your oration into a story with a beginning, middle, and end. You may—and should—expand on your main points, but deliver your speech in an organized, cohesive manner. It will keep you focused on your purpose and keep your audience engaged.

Extemporaneous Speaking

In extemporaneous speaking competitions, an individual blindly selects a current events question and then has thirty minutes to research and prepare a talk on the topic. Rules may differ slightly among tournaments, but individuals generally have five to seven minutes to deliver the speech. Some tournaments require a presentation without notes, and others may allow the speaker to bring an index card with some of their points jotted down for assistance.

The format is challenging. The moment your topic is selected, the clock starts. You must research the topic, identify salient points and gather evidence to support them, outline the framework of your speech along with your persuasive arguments, and then practice delivery. At the end of your thirty minutes, you stand before a panel of judges and present your speech.

It's exhilarating.

And sometimes terrifying.

If you draw a question on the monetary policy of the Federal Reserve, and you aren't really up to speed on the latest financial news, your half-hour research window goes by awfully quickly. Then again, you learn how to think fast on your feet and how to research efficiently. During the preparation time, journal articles, published books, magazines, and newspapers may be consulted, but pre-written notes are prohibited. We used to tote along a few months' (and several pounds') worth of *Time*, *Newsweek,* and the *New York Times* to each tournament. Today, some contests permit the use of the internet during the preparation period, but others will still only allow the use of hard copy evidence.

Outside of the competition walls, extemp skills come in handy. Depending on your occupation, it can be common to have to scramble to put together a brief presentation for your colleagues. If you get involved with the local PTA, you may have to come up to speed quickly on the education budget before speaking to the school board. Heck, if you want an increase in allowance, you need to do some quick research to make compelling and concise arguments to your parents.

Practice enough and extemp will teach you how to process information quickly and articulate your ideas. Similar to an original oratory, extemp requires you to think about what you want your audience to know. If you are asked to speak on the withdrawal of US troops from Afghanistan, do you want to persuade the audience on the positive or negative aspects of the action? Or do you want to explain how the United States came to its policy decision? Either approach works, but the point is to determine why you are addressing this subject.

The framework for an extemp speech is similar to one for original oratory. You have the introduction, where you need to repeat the question you selected and state how you plan to respond to it. Then you should make three to five brief points backed by evidence. The conclusion should support your position on the question.

Let's take the question, "Should cannabis be regulated in the United States?" as an example. You have decided to answer the question affirmatively. Here's an outline of what your speech might look like:

Introduction. You've likely seen it all around you: CBD, or cannabidiol, a derivative of cannabis, may be in your shampoo, your gummy bears, and your afternoon tea. It's not the same as its sister agent, THC, the hallucinogen that gets you high, but its safety and efficacy are unknown. Should cannabis be regulated in the United States? Given the evidence at this point—or the lack thereof—the answer is a resounding yes.

Points. The medical effects of cannabis have been documented. According to the FDA, the US agency responsible for ensuring the safety of many products we consume, CBD has the potential to harm you. CBD can cause liver damage or interact negatively with certain prescription drugs. Using CBD with alcohol may slow brain activity before you become aware of it, leading to unintended drowsiness or sedation. According to the FDA, studies show male animals exposed to CBD have experienced damage to reproductive organs. Since there is little governmental oversight of CBD, the public is exposed to these harms, sometimes unknowingly.

The long-term effects of CBD are not well documented. If you use CBD on a regular basis over a period of days, months, or years, what is the impact on your body and your mental health? Will a weekly shampoo with a CBD additive impact your brain, or would it have no effect? How would ingesting a large quantity twice daily affect your gastrointestinal system? Robust scientific evidence is needed to provide answers to these questions. A regulatory approach would ensure the collection and evaluation of such data, which may then be applied appropriately to the manufacturing process through new rules.

The quality of some CBD products is undetermined. Since there is no required framework to follow, some CBD products may contain harmful toxins, contaminants, and pesticides. One may argue that more reputable companies use accredited laboratories, thus providing assurance that quality techniques and measurements are used, but accreditation is currently voluntary for CBD laboratories.

Only one CBD product, a prescription drug used to treat seizures associated with tuberous sclerosis complex and certain rare forms of epilepsy, has been approved by the FDA. It is illegal to market CBD as a food additive or dietary supplement. Yet there are CBD products that are marketed with unproven medical claims. The FDA has sent warning letters to companies making these and other claims, including one such letter in 2021 that noted significant violations of manufacturing practices.

Conclusion. These concerns, from lack of quality processing to unproven medical claims, are serious and may be assuaged by placing CBD products within a regulatory framework at the FDA. However, that's not to say that CBD is bad or that it does not work. In truth, there is simply a lack of evidence to support it at this time. There are published case studies showing individuals with certain types of pain feel better after a CBD-enhanced cream is rubbed over their skin. This is important information, but it cannot supersede the need for proven safe and efficacious products. The public deserves this protection. The next time you're tempted to nibble some chocolate laced with CBD thinking it will calm your nerves, it would be better to chill in another way until regulatory oversight kicks in.

This example provides you with a general outline of an extemporaneous speech. You can see the structure of an introduction, main points, and conclusion. To strengthen your arguments, cite published evidence or quote from experts in the field.

If appropriate to your talk, you may also explain an opposing view as one of your points and then take a moment to refute it. Using the above model, you might say that some adults report cannabis has been an effective treatment to alleviate chronic pain. You might counter this by acknowledging that the plant has indeed been used for medicinal purposes for centuries, but that does not prove its effectiveness. There's a saying that an apple a day keeps the doctor away, but not many of us survive on an apple-a-day diet. A 1999 Institute of Medicine report titled "Marijuana and Medicine: Assessing the Science Base" recommended that "research should continue into the physiological effects of synthetic and plant-derived cannabinoids and the natural function of cannabinoids found in the body."[viii]

There are a limitless number of topics that may be drawn for extemp. Here are several examples:

Should the US regulate on-line hate speech?

How can the US health system address unconscious bias?

What is restorative justice and should it be employed?

What policy steps should be taken to reduce the impacts of climate change?

What is Havana syndrome and is it a threat to international relations?

Where should the US focus its foreign policy?

Should public transportation be free?

What's the difference between affordable housing and housing that is affordable?

North Korea: engage or ignore?

Should the US and Cuba normalize relations?

What must the Democratic Party do to attract new voters?

What must the Republican Party do to attract new voters?

Is a college education obsolete?

Which new technologies will change the world?

Should cryptocurrency be regulated?

What should cities do to encourage healthy behaviors?

What do rural communities need to survive?

Is Hollywood's influence waning?

Is work-from-home the new economy?

Are noise abatement policies needed in the US?

Will gun control deter crime?

Are Amazon, Apple, and Google too big?

Does fashion matter?

Is public art important?

Similarly, there are endless topics that may come up in daily life that require you to present well-founded arguments. Extemp is not just for competition.

In a meeting with an association, an executive team deliberated on ways to grow and develop the organization's staff. A brainstorm of ideas mostly focused on how to advance people in traditional ways. After a while, one of the quieter members of the group spoke up. He explained how, in order to retain staff, the organization needed to meet people where they were. He outlined, off the cuff, a few points to support his premise. He noted that not all staff wanted to become managers, and some people might still serve the association well by becoming knowledge experts. He argued that the organization needed to incentivize other pathways in order to keep talent. Without knowing it, he presented a concise extemp speech. His colleagues took note and incorporated his ideas into the team's final recommendations.

In another example, the sales and marketing team of a corporation met for a retreat. Before the lunch break, the chief sales officer assigned a task to two of his associates who disagreed over the viability of a product launch. Over the lunch break, each had to prepare a concise, persuasive presentation on their views. These extemporaneous speeches were presented to the full group after lunch and were used by the team in its decision-making.

A form of extemp speaking is used also in social clubs, whether it's called that or not. Perhaps your community pool is considering its annual budget, and you're driving over to the finance committee meeting coming up with ways to convince them to give raises to the lifeguards. You're thinking of an introduction (e.g., *We need to pay our lifeguards well*) and main points (e.g., *Our lifeguards will leave because other pools pay higher wages*; *Our lifeguards, who are trained in CPR, are highly valued*; and *The pool may have to close if we do not have enough lifeguards*), and then a conclusion (e.g., *In conclusion, a 3 percent raise is worth the safety of our members*).

Whether you are in school, the workforce, or just everyday life, opportunities to present an extemp speech will always be there. Extemporaneous speaking enhances your ability to think critically and analytically, and to present smoothly. It also enriches your understanding of current events and other topical matters.

Impromptu

Impromptu is another forensics competition event that translates well into daily life. In impromptu competition, a topic is selected, and then you have about five minutes to prepare what you want to say before you deliver the speech. While your speech should still follow a general framework of an introduction, main points, and a conclusion, the talk need not be persuasive or oriented to a current event. In fact, impromptu speaking may be about almost anything, funny or serious.

I like to think about impromptu speaking the same way one may be asked to give a toast at a special event. You might not have prepared for it, but there you are, standing in a room while one of your best buddies is celebrating a special occasion. The emcee asks you—the best buddy—to say a few words. You can't say no, and you don't want to sound foolish, so impromptu speaking kicks in.

You might say, "I'm so proud of Ralph. When we were growing up, I knew he was destined for greatness. He could always run faster and climb higher than anyone. Of course, it was because he was trying to escape punishment for some devilish deed. Ralph was smart. He knew if he stopped by my house around five p.m. on Fridays, my dad would invite him to stay for pizza night. Ralph was also strategic. He knew that the best time to drop news on his mom was when she was driving. This was how he broke it to her that he wanted to go to West Point. His mom was hesitant at first, but she gripped that steering wheel hard while she navigated the highway and his news. So here we are today, congratulating my friend Ralph for being the fastest, the smartest, the most strategic officer-and-a-gentleman to graduate from West Point. Please join me in celebrating his accomplishments."

One of the fun things about practicing for impromptu competition is that just about anything can be a trigger for your talk. Let's say your prompt is a photo of a chair at a local coffee shop. Your talk might be about how much use that chair has gotten. You might describe the types of people who have sat there, and the types of drinks they ordered. You could conclude by saying that you hope the smart ghosts of coffee chair past rub off on you as you sit there studying for an exam.

Another prompt might encourage a historic talk. If the photo is of a cherry tree, you could begin by musing what the tree would be like if George Washington hadn't chopped it down. The rest of your talk might focus on the benefits of trees, especially cherry ones.

Perhaps your prompt will be a nursery rhyme or a famous quote. If you select the nursery rhyme "Ring Around the Rosy," you might hum a few bars in the beginning but then describe that the true meaning of the popular baby song is not so gleeful. You could then discuss how folklore attributes the rhyme to the Great Plague.

If given President John F. Kennedy's quote, "Ask not what your country can do for you—ask what you can do for your country," you might suggest how that quote applies to the modern era.

Here are some additional prompts to get you going:
  Drum set
  Double Dutch jump rope
  Parking meter
  Quinceañera dress

Ambulance with flashing lights

Tesla Cybertruck

Political candidate sign

Surgical mask

Yarmulke

Tractor

Lincoln Memorial

City lights

Galaxy

"As he read, I fell in love the way you fall asleep: slowly, and then all at once."—*The Fault in Our Stars* by John Green

"Nowadays people know the price of everything and the value of nothing."—Oscar Wilde

"Anyone who ever gave you confidence, you owe them a lot."—Truman Capote

"It was the best of times, it was the worst of times."—*Tale of Two Cities* by Charles Dickens

"After all, tomorrow is another day."—*Gone with the Wind* by Margaret Mitchell

"It doesn't matter who you are or what you look like, so long as somebody loves you."—Roald Dahl

Eiffel Tower

Olympic rings

Elephants

Rotary dial phone

Balloons

Readings and Interpretations

Reading aloud or interpreting the written word orally may sometimes be taken for granted. With the prevalence of podcasts and audiobooks, one might think it's a common skill, but it's not. Being read to out loud is something that many of us have experienced from birth. *Pat the Bunny* by Dorothy Kunhardt, *Goodnight Moon* by Margaret Wise Brown, and other children's tales are recited to help children process language as well as coax them to sleep. Yet readings and interpretations take on a somewhat different magnitude when presented as a public speaking skill.

The genres vary: prose or poetry reading; dramatic, humorous, or duet interpretations; storytelling; and more. They each represent an art form for expressing thoughts through written words. Speakers use published works, which may come from novels, poems, essays, biographies, short stories, journals or anthologies. It's not acting—there are no costumes or props— but good speakers have the ability to transport the audience. By using their voice, they convey the meaning of the piece as well as its characters and tone.

Readings are just that: readings. Whether in competition or reciting from a published novel at a coffee shop, the speaker will use and refer to a manuscript while presenting. Prose and poetry readings are not memorized. Interpretations, however, may need to be memorized, depending on the tournament rules. Interpretative speakers may use movement, but motions and gestures should be restrained for memorized storytelling or myths.

Think of what you want to express. If you have a knack for mimicking others, a dramatic or humorous interpretation may be a great way to exhibit and refine your skills. Find that piece that allows you to portray the voice of an old man, old woman, monster, or baby. But remember, interpretation is more than a stand-up routine. You need to understand the piece you are expressing so that the audience will find a meaning as well.

The same is true for duet interpretations. Generally, the two speakers do not look at one another when performing; instead, they project their characters to the audience. (Remember, not acting here!) Imagine you (duo partner #1) are whispering passionate thoughts into the ear of your lover (duo partner #2). You won't actually be whispering into their ear. You'll be looking away from your partner and uttering that affection out toward the audience. It's a learned talent.

Often, people want to duet with their bestie. I'm not going to interfere in your personal life, but give this some thought. Sometimes it's easier to strike the right chord with someone you don't know as well. There are a few examples that we won't mention here of brilliant actors who have zero on-screen chemistry with their significant others. Off-screen they may sizzle, but not on film. I liken this to ballroom dancing. In my dance class, the instructor will ask everyone to switch partners every fifteen minutes or so. No matter who you came with, you have to dance with everyone. Since you and your partner are already familiar with each other's habits and personalities, dancing with someone else teaches you new and better dance moves. It's the same with duet interpretations. Give someone else a try.

So what literary work should you use? There are limitless examples of published works you may review in preparing to speak. Are you into sports? There's *I Never Had It Made* by Jackie Robinson or *Sandy Koufax: A Lefty's Legacy* by Jane Leavy for baseball fans. There's *The Blind Side* by Michael Lewis or *How Soccer Explains the World* by Franklin Foer for the footballers, American or otherwise. If you enjoy fables, both light and dark, there is *Hans Andersen's Fairy Tales* by Hans Christian Andersen, *The Gift of the Magi* by O. Henry, or *Ogresse*, a vivid panorama of a flesh-eating monster who falls in love, by Grammy awardwinning vocalist and composer Cécile McLorin Salvant. If you recite a parable, you need to determine the moral of the story and express it well in your presentation.

For stories that provide an anthropological look at segments of society, read *Mules and Men* by Zora Neale Hurston or *The*

Kandy-Kolored Tangerine-Flake Streamline Baby by Tom Wolfe. If you're interested in romance, there's *Sense and Sensibility* by Jane Austen, *Love Story* by Erich Segal, or *The Fault in Our Stars* by John Green. Plays like *Death of a Salesman* by Arthur Miller, *The Odd Couple* by Neil Simon, and *A Raisin in the Sun* by Lorraine Hansberry may pique your interest. Books by Barbara Kingsolver, Harper Lee, F. Scott Fitzgerald, Christopher Buckley, Jhumpa Lahiri, Truman Capote, James McBride, J.D. Salinger, Philip Roth, William Shakespeare, Chimamanda Ngozi Adichie, Frank McCourt, and so many, many more are all there for exploring. When you find a book that sings to you and your interests, it's likely a good place to begin thinking of how to speak its words.

I'm serious about that "sings to you" advice. For interpretations, you needn't find the most dramatic—or overdramatic—literature, nor should you necessarily seek the knee-slapping, guffaw-inducing humorous ones either. Pick something that matches you and your sensibilities. You'll likely portray its meaning all the better and capture the audience's attention, which is key. Drama and humor can be tough customers. One person's blood and guts and gore are another's upset stomach. Juvenile pieces filled with bathroom humor may turn off a roomful of adults. Select your pieces accordingly.

The selected work is usually edited to fit within a time frame. A speaker will not interpret Victor Hugo's *Les Misérables* by reading all of *Les Misérables*, but they may find a meaningful passage to convey. One poem may be too short to have an impact as a presentation, so a speaker might use a published collection of poems by the same author.

Whether you plan to recite or interpret in competition or in a less formal setting like at a café, bookstore, social club, or senior center, check on the rules. The National Speech and Debate Association is an excellent source for the latest rules for high school competitions. On the collegiate level, the American Forensic Association and other groups, universities, and conferences put forth tournament instructions.

Local communities host speaking events, and they have guidelines too. Busboys and Poets, a restaurant in Washington, DC, hosts general open mic poetry nights, and the Nuyorican Poets Café is famous in New York City for its weekly slams. Towns across the world from Greenville, South Carolina, to St. Louis, Missouri, to Brussels, Belgium, to Addis Ababa, Ethiopia, attract audiences for their original poetry reads. Sometimes oratory competitions are held in conjunction with special festivals or holidays. Ethnic heritage festivals, Juneteenth, Independence Day, and Veterans Day all present opportunities to recite the written word. Time limits, speaking genre, and type of presentation may vary depending on the setting. You might be permitted to read the words of others or encouraged to present a self-authored piece.

Chapter Five

Gain Life Skills

Any one of these styles of speaking will improve your oratory skills, but the experience you amass runs much deeper. You will learn how to speak up and present yourself to the public, but you will also acquire and enhance other life skills, such as researching, critical thinking, organizing, note-taking, and editing.

Do the Research

It may seem obvious, but to deliver an extemporaneous speech, you need to have a command of current events. This requires poring over newspapers, magazines, and academic journals. To debate a policy question, you have to explore numerous sources to understand all sides of the issue. Even if you present a prose reading, you first need to decide what to recite. All of these activities involve research.

We're talking about more than just looking up the answer to a question you don't know. Research for a public speech, especially one on current events or policy, prepares you to know the subject matter well. You will become a less hesitant speaker once you have gathered a core of knowledge from which to draw.

To make your research efforts productive, identify the specific item you want to learn more about and explain in your speech. You need to determine what information you actually want to seek. While I'm all for infinite reading and knowledge-seeking (hey, I'm one of those people who read the encyclopedia as a child), for speech-giving or debate purposes, you need to hone in on your subject matter.

Consider these examples: Do you want to give a speech on electric vehicles or on the comparison of electric vehicles to gas-powered vehicles, or on electric vehicle mileage range, or on the environmental impact of electric vehicles? While each speech would require some knowledge of electric vehicles, the specific topic provides direction for your research. Maybe your speech on electric vehicles would inform the audience of the companies that are producing them and the types of car models anticipated in the marketplace. On the other hand, your comparison speech might focus on the cost to produce an electric vehicle versus a gas-powered vehicle. The point is, your speech could be all over the place unless you focus your information gathering.

While it's paramount to figure out exactly what you want to speak about, it might not be that simple. It's common to first state a premise and then go research all the facts to support your idea. Yet it helps to walk into research with an open mind. You may start to gather data only to find that the focus of your speech needs to change. That's perfectly fine. You may also have a general sense of what you want to talk about—let's say "horses"—but you have no clue how to approach the subject. In this case, you might gather lots of material on horses: evolution of horses, different breeds, how to ride, proper care, sports betting, mythology, and diet. After browsing through a variety of information, you may then determine the specific approach to your speech.

Sometimes, when you say the word "research," people imagine entering an esteemed laboratory or conducting a detailed statistical analysis. That's not the meaning of research here. Doing research for a speech means searching widely for facts, figures, and opinions. You are essentially conducting an investigation to obtain information.

Here's how to do it. Start reading—a lot. Get your hands on scientific journals, trade magazines, policy briefs, and books. Read newspapers, especially major publications like the *New York Times*, the *Washington Post*, and the *Wall Street Journal*. For topical intelligence, read in-depth analyses in magazines like the *Atlantic*, the *Economist*, *Foreign Affairs*, and *Science*. There are all sorts of specialty publications that will broaden your horizons. Depending on your area of focus, you might read *Flying Magazine*, *Planning Magazine*, *Vogue*, or *Nature*. I like reading community newspapers to gain new perspectives. The *Sun Gazette*, my hometown paper, prints reflective editorials on local topics. *ArlNow.com* is an online news outlet in Arlington, Virginia, that includes an open forum filled with opinions ranging from crass to insightful. It almost doesn't matter what you read—just read!

As you embark on reading, start considering the credibility of your research materials and begin to root out bias. It's actually okay if a source is biased, as long as you recognize that slant. For example, some news articles may seem authoritative about a new diet scheme, but if you look at the top of the article, the words "sponsored advertisement" appear. This means that someone was paid to write an article with a particular viewpoint. This fact alone does not mean the information is bad, but you should be cognizant that a specific viewpoint is being levied. When a cotton candy manufacturer writes an article about the positive health benefits of cotton candy, questions will arise about its validity. Yet if a national dental association writes that cotton candy, eaten once or twice a year, will not harm you, then you likely have a source with less bias.

Basically, you want the information you are gathering to be strong enough to support your premise. You can do this by asking yourself several questions.

Is the information relevant to your point? It may seem obvious, but if you're giving a talk on the harmful effects of caffeine on the human nervous system, don't cite a study that concludes moderate coffee intake has health benefits.

Is the information timely? Look at the date of the publication and determine if the material is relevant. I shake my head whenever someone argues a medical procedure is too new for hospital use and cites thirty-year-old literature to "prove" it.

Is the information accurate? Examine the details of your evidence to ensure that the information is depicted accurately. If your speech is advocating for housing affordability, you need to define and articulate what is affordable. Blankly stating 15 percent of your town's total housing stock is affordable is not accurate if you haven't created other metrics around that number. Is housing affordability defined as housing that costs 30 percent of the area median income or 80 percent? The percent of total housing stock that is considered affordable will fluctuate depending on your response.

Is the information from an authoritative source? There are several public databases that may be combed for scholarly works, including PubMed.gov, JSTOR.org, Scopus.com, and EBSCO.com. Other sites, such as SCImagoJR.com and scholar.google.com, provide impact and quality rankings for various journals.

Wikipedia and some other internet sources may have juicy details, but, because the information is crowdsourced, its authenticity may be questionable. Quoting "evidence" from a friend's Facebook page is also likely not a credible source. The same is true for randomly stating that "most people think (insert a claim)" when you have no statistics to back up the assertion. Go ahead and read Wikipedia and Reddit and Facebook, but be sure to read the fine print. On Wikipedia, for example, there is usually a reference section at the end of each page. That's your gold mine. Go ahead and check the references. That's where you may find an accurate, original source.

Searches on the internet may lead to links to random pages, chat rooms, and malware bots. For example, look up information on pancreatic cancer. Sources like the American Cancer Society, Mayo Clinic, and the National Institutes of Health are more credible and less biased than pages that are flagged as ads or chats. A peer-reviewed study will usually carry more weight than an article in a popular monthly magazine. Information procured from regulated websites that have domain names ending in, .gov or .mil, for example, will usually be more reliable than material from sites that have no oversight or review.

Some evidence is better than others. Quantifiable evidence obtained from a randomized controlled trial carries more weight than the opinion of one person. Let's use the fictitious example of PudgyLips, a lipstick that boasts the ability to double the size of your lips in thirty days. An independent government laboratory tested the lipstick claim on one hundred women ages 18-24 for a period of thirty days. Half of the women were asked to wear PudgyLips daily and the other half were asked to wear a generic moisturizing lipstick daily. None of the women knew which lipstick they were testing. At the end of the trial period, 65 percent of the women testing PudgyLips thought their lips looked somewhat swollen but none of the participants thought their lips had doubled in size. Of the women testing the generic lipstick, 57 percent thought their lips were slightly swollen, but none thought that their lips had doubled in size. The trial scientists measured the lips of the women before and after the experiment and found no discernible difference. On the other hand, you saw a social media post with a teen influencer who swears by the doubled plumpness of her lips after using PudgyLips. Which information do you believe? What would be most convincing to your listening audience?

My great-aunt swore that by eating seven almonds a day she would ward off future arthritis. This self-prescribed treatment had no scientific foundation to support it. There were no journal articles weighing whether any of the nutrients in almonds fights arthritis or the benefits of five almonds versus seven or twelve. There was no expert consensus panel from a national rheumatology society recommending a seven-almonds-a-day treatment. The National Institute of Arthritis and Musculoskeletal and Skin Diseases (NIAMSD) is silent on the matter. It would be rather dubious for your speech on arthritis to state that seven almonds a day are all the prevention you need without the requisite research and evidence. Quoting my great-aunt's words from a chat room, as intelligent as she was, would not be credible evidence for your speech on arthritis.

Instead, you might discuss home remedies that exist for arthritis prevention, including the seven-a-day plan. You would need to state whether these remedies are supported by scientific evidence. You might quote a prominent source, like NIAMSD, as saying that almonds are a calcium-rich food that may improve your health, but that a seven-a-day plan is not rooted in scientific discovery.

In addition to reading, talk to people. Identify individuals who are knowledgeable on the subject you are researching. Ask to speak with them to help broaden your own understanding of the topic. The purpose is not to quote them in your speech (you're not a journalist), but to learn from them.

Unless you already know the person you want to interview, this will require a bit of homework. You must identify the person, figure out how to approach them, and then decide what to say.

Renowned composer and lyricist Stephen Sondheim publicly and frequently credited another famed lyricist, Oscar Hammerstein II for influencing his career. A young Sondheim lived near Hammerstein and his family. As a teenager, Sondheim wrote a musical which Hammerstein critiqued. This relationship and those words helped shape his career.

Of course, not all of us have access to such notable talent. We can, however, reach out to those more knowledgeable than ourselves.

There are many ways to identify an individual with whom you may wish to speak. Consider first who you already know. Are there teachers, colleagues, neighbors, relatives, or friends who know about your selected subject matter? If you already have an established relationship, starting a conversation is easier.

I enjoy gardening. Honestly, I mostly enjoy planting and watering flowers and vegetables and watching them grow. I have no patience for learning the various species of plants, soil compositions, and ideal growth conditions. Before I make an investment in a plant, I ask my master gardener friends how large the plant might get or if it will bloom in full sun. The local nursery usually has someone on the grounds who doles out similar advice. This is how I gather gardening information.

If you don't have these types of connections, look at ones you might be able to establish. Review what you have researched already. Does the information you've collected frequently reference certain people or institutions? Are there organizations, especially local ones, that may proffer expertise on the subject? Is there a friend of a friend who may know someone to help? Ask if they'll make an introduction for you.

Think of it this way: If you are planning a speech on physical therapy and you don't know any physical therapists, have you searched online for "physical therapists near me"? Are there other physicians you know (your family doctor, for example) who might be able to recommend names of local physical therapists? If this doesn't work, consider reaching out to a national physical therapy association and checking the names of physical therapists who sit on its board or publish articles. You might ask the association's public affairs office directly for names of individuals who may be able to assist you.

If you are compiling research for a debate and have questions about behavioral economics, look for names of professors that are mentioned in your research. Check the reference section of books you have read to get ideas. While it may be thrilling and intellectually stimulating to ask a Nobel Prize winner in economics to answer your questions, it's likely not necessary. Consider identifying graduate students or lecturers on the matter instead.

Once you identify the names of people who may be able to assist or mentor you, what do you really know about them? You need to do some research here too.

Let's say you're preparing a speech or debate on the impact of reality television on American society. You've decided that it would be helpful to communicate with a reality television producer. Calling up the network and asking to speak with the producer of *America's Got Talent*, for example, will get you absolutely nowhere.

What do you know about the producer, and why would the person want to speak with you? You should know the name of the producer and have an understanding of their background and what they do for a living. Resources like LinkedIn may help you discover their professional experiences and how tenured they are in the television production profession. Do they belong to certain clubs or organizations? Where did they go to school? What other shows have they produced? Have articles been written about them? Have they written articles on the subject about which you are planning to speak? All of this information will help you form a better understanding of the person you want to interview. If you have commonalities (Did you graduate from the same college? Were they also on the debate team in high school?), there's a better chance that the producer will want to communicate with you.

As you develop a clearer picture of the individual, figure out what you want to discuss. There's nothing like meeting someone who may be willing to assist you and finding yourself tongue-tied or nonplussed.

Take, for example, a friend of mine who entered an office building elevator and found Broadway and television star Taye Diggs inside. My friend said, "Mr. Diggs, may I introduce you to my daughter?" Her preteen daughter, an acting aspirant, looked up at Mr. Diggs nonchalantly. My friend wanted to impress upon her daughter that she was meeting acting royalty and started to list Mr. Diggs' accomplishments. The daughter was pleasant but seemed unimpressed. Then my friend told her that Mr. Diggs was married to Idina Menzel. "Idina Menzel!" yelled the young girl. "I love her!!" Mr. Diggs laughed good-naturedly and said he couldn't wait to tell his wife.

Be ready for opportunities and chance encounters. In preparation for your talk, what do you want to ask someone that you haven't learned from your research? Do you want to understand better the behavioral economics behind a five-cent tax on plastic grocery bags? Do you want to know why producers select certain guests for reality shows? Is there a distinction between physical therapists and personal fitness trainers? What inspired you to get into acting? You need to do your homework and ask the right questions to elicit a useful response.

Basically, if you speak with others about your speech topic, think about what you want to learn from them. They may impart knowledge that you never considered.

Think about professional speechwriters, the people who write speeches for other people. They need to understand both the subject matter and the person for whom they are drafting a speech. David Litt, a speechwriter for President Barack Obama, in an interview about his book, *Thanks, Obama: My Hopey Changey White House Years*, explained that it was important to meld the technical policy side of a speech with an engaging narrative. Sarah Hurwitz, chief speechwriter for First Lady Michelle Obama, has explained how she felt at home in the first lady's voice and liked what Mrs. Obama was speaking about. Writers who draft monologues for late-night television hosts must understand the personality of the host. They also must have a good grasp of current events and a sense of humor. These professionals are constantly researching and writing so that the speakers they write for may deliver strong monologues.

As you're doing your research, consider, too, Sir Isaac Newton's third law of motion: "For every action, there is an equal and opposite reaction." The material you gather should show various perspectives. Finding information that supports your point of view is only part of the equation. To be an effective speaker or debater, you need to understand the opposing views, be able to state them, and try to refute them. There will always be opposing views that may equal yours in weight.

If you give a speech about puppies and all you talk about is how lovable and adorable they are, it might engender warm feelings from those listening. Yet some people may be listening to you talk, and all they can think about is how their neighbor's puppy chewed their favorite sweater to shreds. Your speech on the lovability of puppies might be more impressive if you acknowledge the opposing view and then refute it. You might say, "As sweet as they are, puppies can also be mischievous. My puppy has ruined a sofa and a patch of carpet, yet puppies have been shown to improve the mental health and well-being of their humans. A study by the Mid-Regional Center for Veterinary Research found the health benefits outweigh the cost of minor cosmetic damage." Of course, this is a fictitious example. Your research would find studies from legitimate sources and cite them as needed.

Research also applies to oral readings and interpretations. Rare is the occasion when you just pick up a book and read a passage aloud as your selection. Depending on your public speaking category, you'll need to read a few novels, short stories, poems, or plays before finding one that suits you. You might have an author in mind, like Michael Lewis or Sinclair Lewis, but which of their writings will you select? You may decide that drama is for you—but there's a lot of drama out there from which to choose. Reviewing authors and their literary works is another form of research.

Research is a skill set that will serve you well in school, in business and in life. If your refrigerator is on the fritz, do you just go buy another one, or do you look into the price and value of various brands? Do you find out which store has a sale on the brand you prefer? That's research.

Do you have a blind date with your best friend's cousin? I bet you Google his name to see where he's from and what he does. Did your boss ask you to give a presentation on sales figures for the third quarter? Yep, research is involved.

Take Note

As you conduct your research, you need to keep track of important citations, sources, and facts. No matter the type of speaking you plan to do, you need a system for categorizing your materials. If you give an original presentation on how to plant a tree, you might organize your information in the following categories: soil types, planting zones, tree characteristics, and effective tips. Under each category, list the source of the information (e.g., *Horticulture* magazine, Purdue Extension, US Department of Agriculture) and then a specific citation (e.g., author, title, and date) and an internet link. It's smart to create a bibliography of sources that you use in the speech so you can properly acknowledge and reference them.

You should expect to collect a lot more information than you will actually use in your speech or debate. All of this research will help make you a more informed presenter. Take note of the information for future reference; it isn't necessary to memorize all the data and details. Plan on stockpiling an abundance of material from which you may choose the information most relevant and powerful for your talk. Keep in mind, this mass of material may also help you answer questions that may be posed by the audience.

For extemporaneous speaking, I used to carry around the latest editions of *Newsweek* and *Time* as part of my research materials. Having read the articles in advance, I could reference them at a glance if the subject matter warranted it.

If you are debating an issue, consider organizing your research by arguments. Divide the material into two parts: one that supports the affirmative position and one that supports the negative. Then further subdivide the information by the case you wish to support. Let's say you are debating the question, "Should parents be held accountable for crimes their children commit?" One set of materials would support arguments in favor of the proposition and the other set would support the opposite. Your materials might be further separated by type of crime, age of the child, parental oversight styles, child psychology, and parental involvement in the crime. This system will help you organize your research and your thoughts.

Office aids can also make note-taking more distinctive for you. Each subheading might be coded in a different color for quick reference. File folders with tabs on the right might contain your affirmative arguments and folders with left tabs would house the opposite. A long legal pad is helpful for creating a flow chart of arguments in the margin of the page. Keep all your material in one place—whether in a file cabinet, brief case, or stack—so it's easier to find.

Keep it Pithy

Fitting a speech or reading into a time requirement will help you learn editing skills. Learning to edit will not only make you a better public speaker, it will also enhance your writing abilities.

A bright and talented student from the George Washington University, Kathleen, interned with my office many years ago. Her assignments included reviewing regulations and listening to congressional hearings. With each assignment, she was tasked with writing a summary of her findings. She would regularly come into my office with several pages of single-spaced memos. She spent considerable time conscientiously capturing all the details. I would take a quick glance at each memo and say, "I'm not reading this."

She'd shoot me an incredulous look. "What? Why not?"

I would explain that I didn't have time to absorb all these details. That's why she had the assignment, not me. I wanted a pared down version that captured the important points. It often took a few tries, but eventually Kathleen could whip out detailed one-page memos that told me everything I needed to know on the matter at hand.

Years later, when she became a naval officer, she told me that her superiors often commended her for her ability to concisely and accurately make her points. She said it was my one-page memo demand that taught her that skill.

Now, we're talking about speeches here, not one-page memos, but the skill set is the same. When discussing a topic, whether in an original oration or an extemporaneous one, you need to be succinct to be most effective. Making your point and moving on to the next one is better than a belabored (and likely boring) oration.

Take the time to read your draft speech over and over again with an eye for what to edit. You are looking to see if any sentences or ideas are repeated and if the speech flows smoothly. For example:

A disruption in the nation's supply chain is causing a shortage of basic household items. It is difficult to find paper towels, disinfectant spray, and disposable cups.

These two sentences would become more succinct if edited together, such as:

A disruption in the nation's supply chain is making it difficult to obtain paper towels, disinfectant spray, disposable cups, and other basic household items.

Or if you are making three points in your speech about the importance of trees in a city environment, are those points distinct enough? Let's say your points are that trees: 1) are good for the environment, 2) help fight carbon dioxide, and 3) absorb pollutants. Point number one is redundant when included with the others. Your speech is about how trees are good for a city environment, and that premise should be captured in the introduction and conclusion of your speech. Making it a point unto itself is redundant and less persuasive.

Edit it. Instead, add points that better support the premise by stating that trees: 1) cool city temperatures, 2) help fight carbon dioxide, and 3) absorb pollutants.

If you are giving an impromptu or extemporaneous speech, you may feel an urge to fill your speech with redundant phrases. It will take practice, but you should work toward stating your point once and well. Think of how many times you've heard someone "raise a glass" to cheer someone on and they say, "Billy is a great guy. He's always there for us. Everyone loves him. Let's toast our great man, Billy." No one disputes that Billy is super or that the toast is sincere, but with some simple editing, "Let's raise our glasses to toast Billy, a loyal friend to us all" would do the trick.

Editing is important, too, when reciting prose or poetry. When this is someone else's work (give credit to the author!), you may not insert your own language, no matter how much you think it will improve your reading. Despite this rule, the flow of the recitation must make sense.

Take, for example, the novel *The Jungle*, written by Upton Sinclair in 1906, which portrays the struggles and gruesome working conditions of immigrants in the United States. Below is an excerpt from the acclaimed work:

> Jurgis was like a boy, a boy from the country. He was the sort of man the bosses like to get hold of, the sort they make it a grievance they cannot get hold of. When he was told to go to a certain place, he would go there on the run. When he had nothing to do for the moment, he would stand round fidgeting, dancing, with the overflow of energy that was in him. If he were working in a line of men, the line always moved too slowly for him, and you could pick him out by his impatience and restlessness. That was why he had been picked out on one important occasion; for Jurgis had stood outside of Brown and Company's "Central Time Station" not more than half an hour, the second day of his arrival in Chicago, before he had been beckoned by one of the bosses. Of this he was very proud, and it made him more disposed than ever to laugh at the pessimists. In vain would they all tell him that there were men in that crowd from which he had been chosen who had stood there a month— yes, many months—and not been chosen yet. "Yes," he would say, "but what sort of men? Broken-down tramps and good-for-nothings, fellows who have spent all their money drinking, and want to get more for it. Do you

want me to believe that with these arms"—and he would clench his fists and hold them up in the air, so that you might see the rolling muscles— "that with these arms people will ever let me starve?"

This novel expresses several themes. In addition to the experiences of immigrants, the novel exposed practices of the US meatpacking industry during the early twentieth century. Does this excerpt portray the theme you wish to reveal? If not, what other sections of the book would you include to complete the thought? When read aloud, does this excerpt fit with your speaking style? To find literature to recite, you need to do some reading and research to understand the prose and then edit a section appropriately to bring across its meaning in a cogent way.

In college, a forensics teammate and I were paired to perform a duo interpretation where we stood side by side and, using only our voices, performed a segment of a play. There were no props or stage movements. We decided to read from *Same Time, Next Year*, a romantic comedy written by Bernard Slade. The gist of the play is that two people have an affair and then, over a period of twenty-five years, meet once a year to rekindle their relationship.

My teammate, a tall, lanky fellow with a mop top of blond hair, and I needed a quiet place to test our reading of the play. We wanted to read whole sections aloud and then decide which components could be used for a brief duet. Meeting at the student union, we found an isolated area on the top floor. We walked down a quiet hallway past several open-air classrooms to find a single bench where we could sit together and practice. There was no one in sight. A perfect setting, we thought.

We started reading aloud and were really getting into it. Deep in concentration, we didn't realize one of the classrooms down the hall had started to fill with students. Our volume grew. We got to a passage where the character, Doris, is pregnant, and George, the other protagonist, touches her belly:

> *George:* When I touched you I started to get excited! What kind of pervert am I? I'm staring at a two-hundred-pound pregnant woman and I'm getting hot!
>
> *Doris:* Well, I'll tell you something, that's the nicest thing anyone's said to me in months.

Suddenly, we heard the classroom burst into laughter. Our trance broken, we stared at each other and realized the students thought we were describing a personal moment. Laughing, yet mortified, we quickly slipped out a back staircase.

We used that excerpt in our duo competition.

Muscle Memory

You've no doubt heard the phrase "speaking without thinking," and I dare say you can point to a number of people who are afflicted with this unfortunate condition. Some refer to it unpleasantly as *diarrhea of the mouth*. They just talk and talk and talk without regard for the words spoken. The skill set of speaking effortlessly on a chosen matter is desirable as long as there is relevance behind it. That leads us to muscle memory.

When giving a public speech, you do not need to memorize it. Yes, there are caveats. If you are participating in an academic forensics competition, the rules may require committing a speech to memory, but there are not many other situations where memorization is mandatory. It's not the point of public speaking to judge how well you recall the words.

I can hear many of you breathing a sigh of relief.

That said, there are times when you may want to speak without notes. In my extemp competitions, I was permitted to refer to notes on an index card, if I so chose. Sometimes I would jot the outline of my speech on the card. Having it handy was like a security blanket. I didn't really need the index card, but it gave me comfort to know that it was there should the words fail me. You can do that too, especially if you have a statistic that must be stated correctly or an exact statement from a source that must be quoted accurately.

Yet even without the rote memorization of a speech, public speaking builds muscle memory. Muscle memory is when an everyday activity is automatic—you do it without thinking. If you rode a bike only as a kid, you likely can push the pedals again at age fifty without taking a lesson. Or have you noticed that you can sit down in front of a computer and begin typing a memo without thinking about the keys in front of you? That's muscle memory.

Public speaking works that way too. With enough practice, your brain will begin to adapt to the comfort of speaking out. You must think before you speak, but the actual activity of speaking up will become routine the more you exercise this muscle.

It should go without saying that you must practice the craft of speaking. It's how you develop any new skill. What I want to impress upon you is how to exercise your muscle memory so that speaking becomes second nature.

To train your brain to perform this way, you need a hack. I have three to offer you. First, you must practice speaking aloud. It's not enough to read and reread your speech. Reading is one skill; speaking is another. If you have a speech or reci-tation that you want to commit to memory, start slow. Read the first paragraph aloud and repeat it several times. Then take a break. Go check your messages, take a nap, eat lunch, what-ever. Just remove yourself from the paragraph. After a short while, pick up the paragraph again and speak it. These mini-recesses will help your brain capture the material.

In practicing, I will often speak my thoughts and then sleep on them. I often dream of myself giving the speech. By morning, I can usually deliver the speech without consciously thinking about it.

You may have no intention of memorizing your talk, but you'll want to remember the process of speaking it. For example, go ahead and recite the alphabet right now. I bet you can do it without looking at any notes. It's as if you're speaking without thinking. This is your muscle memory, and it will help you speak in a smoother, more fluid manner.

If you fall down the stairs and break your arm, you will have to wear a cast for a few weeks. During that time, your arm often forgets how to move. Once the cast is gone, you have to exercise the sore arm repeatedly. Eventually, your muscle should come back and remember how to lift a suitcase and toss a ball. This example applies to your voice too. You need to get used to using it so it remembers what to do.

As for the second hack, use that index card. Before you practice, write down the major elements of your speech on one 4-by-6 inch card. For each section, select one word or phrase as your prompt. Then, as you practice aloud, eschew the formal speech and only reference the index card. At first, your speech may meander a little. It may take you some time to articulate your point, but that's okay. As you exercise your muscle memory with these prompts, you'll be able to recall the body of your speech more clearly.

For an oratory on microloans, your index card might look like this:

A. Story
B. Define
   1. Mohammad Yunus, Grameen
   2. $500-$100,000
C. Entrepreneurs
D. Poverty alleviation
   1. United Nations, 10 percent at/below extreme poverty

        in 2015
    E. How/where
    F. Conclude

This card will tell you to begin with a personal story about microlending. It will prompt you to explain to the audience what microloans are and to credit Nobel Prize winner Mohammad Yunus for establishing the Grameen Bank and the amount of a typical loan. Your next three prompts outline the main points you wish to make: how microloans help entrepreneurs and the economy; how microlending has alleviated poverty; and how/where/when to obtain a microloan. The card then instructs you to provide your closing thoughts.

Likely, you have already written your full speech, but you won't read it verbatim. Instead, the index card prompts are all you need. Eventually, you likely won't need the card either. This way you haven't memorized your speech, but you are *giving* a speech. You will have more command of your presentation and be more engaging to the listener.

If you are still concerned about remembering parts of your speech, you may be interested in this third hack. Develop an introduction and closing that you may use no matter the situation or speech. For example, your introduction might always begin with a story about your neighbor's kid and the conclusion will always explain what happened to the child. Or you might always begin your talk with the same special quote and then close by explaining how your speech relates to that quote.

A number of political candidates use this technique. They always begin by introducing themselves to the audience with words like: "I know this community like the back of my hand. I was born at the local hospital—thanks, Mom!—and went to our fine public schools. I'll admit my initials were etched into the big oak near the football bleachers during high school. When it comes to public education, I understand our schools from the inside out." The candidate will use this same introduction throughout the campaign. The main points of the speech will change to meet the needs of the audience, but the opening words have been seared in the candidate's brain.

Some candidates use the same technique in closing statements. Some will repeat the same phrase, no matter the context of the speech, to leave the audience with a sense of inspiration. "Together, we will soar" is one such phrase that is easy to memorize and may apply to many speeches.

While this particular hack may help you commit certain portions of your speech to memory, it can get stale quickly for both the speaker and the audience. Use it sparingly.

Think Critically

As you are amassing these life skills of researching, note-taking, organizing, editing, and building muscle memory, you are working toward your goal of delivering a public speech. You are figuring out the purpose of your speech and what information supports your decision. You are solving problems and assessing pros and cons—whether in the appropriateness of a prose selection or the points of an extemporaneous argument. You have a goal to achieve, and these life skills will back you in this endeavor. It is a path that may lead to critical thinking.

When used optimally, forensics will engage our abilities to evaluate and analyze a matter, to synthesize information, and to theorize on solutions and approaches. You begin to weigh possibilities and think about a proper course of action. When thinking critically, you look beyond the usual responses and typical assumptions. You seek to understand matters in a broader realm.

It's relatively easy to stand up and say you are for or against an issue. However, most matters aren't black and white. There is a lot of gray to consider when thinking critically.

Look at it this way. A physician tells a patient he has cancer. This is a rather definitive statement. The next steps require more thought. How do you treat the patient? First, you need more information. What type of cancer is it? How advanced is it? Does the patient have certain symptoms? What are the circumstances of the patient? Answers to these and other questions will help determine if the patient should have surgery, radiation, chemotherapy, or wait before taking further action. This is an example of critical thinking.

Now look at critical thinking in the context of debate. You may be asked to argue in the affirmative that bottled water should be banned. Let's say you've accumulated enough evidence to support this argument and you've presented a winning debate. Yet when you think about the matter further, you're not so sure this makes absolute sense. Maybe you agree with some of your opponent's arguments. Maybe you understand that new types of biodegradable material make plastic water bottles less harmful to the environment. Maybe you are concerned about public health conditions during a heat wave or other natural disaster, when it is essential to get water to people quickly and bottled water is the best answer.

These considerations do not mean you are "caving" on your arguments. Life and public policy are rarely so rigid. You are looking more closely at an issue and considering it from different viewpoints. How we synthesize that information and use it to respond is all part of critical thinking.

To exercise this skill, look beyond selective arguments, over-generalizations, and personal biases. Using the example above, perhaps not *all* bottled water is bad. Perhaps bottled water is more than an environmental issue, and is also one of public health and commerce concerns.

Public speaking is an important conduit for critical thinking. One presents arguments and expresses ideas but also learns the opinions of others. Extemporaneous speaking and original oratory allow for various views to be considered and explored. This creates a bridge to more tolerance and solution-building.

Nicholas G. Meriwether, who is featured later in this book, is Director of Museum Planning and Development at the Haight Street Art Center in San Francisco. He recalls, "In high school debate, you would drill down to the heart of any big complex topic, such as international trade or the viability of air bags. Yet the team that won the national competition wasn't particularly right about its issue. Their position was just enormously well researched and enormously well argued. But there was no inherent truth that was revealed, or at least that was just my sense at the time. But that was an important lesson: Debate should be a mirror to good policy, good law."

Forensics offers the right prescription. If we engage in it often enough, we may learn to more impactfully develop and express opinions and beliefs. It may not hasten world peace, but it bodes well for better understanding of differing views.

Chapter Six

Speak!

Grab 'Em at the Start

Now that you know the basic structure for speeches, let's look in more detail at how to get started. A hauntingly beautiful song, "Say Something," written by Ian Axel, Chad King, and Mike Campbell, and made popular with a performance by A Great Big World and Christina Aguilera, tells the story of a dying relationship. It urges the loved one to show their feelings before it's too late. Similarly, with a speech, you need to express yourself before the audience loses interest.

You don't need to tell a joke or story or offer a quote, but you could. You don't have to razzle-dazzle anyone, but you need to speak in a manner that warrants a further listen by your audience.

Some people begin a speech by describing what they are going to discuss. Personally, a speech that begins with a table of contents does not appeal to me. I'm thinking, "Don't waste my time telling me what you are going to talk about; just talk about it already." Summarize your points at the end, if you wish, but don't give me a list at the beginning.

You need to think about how to be interesting. Forget about giving a speech for a moment and think about how you engage in daily life. In the midst of the pandemic in 2020, someone lamented to me that every day seemed like a scene in the movie *Groundhog Day* where she was living the same day over and over again. Yet, despite nothing new happening, it was easy to talk on the phone for hours on end. There must have been something interesting to discuss, even if daily life was mundane.

If you were in an elevator with a stranger and you wanted to start a conversation, what would you say? Would you talk about the weather, ponder the fact that the elevator did not have a button for the thirteenth floor, or wonder aloud why some elevators have televisions in them? You might compliment the stranger on their jacket or ask for suggestions for a near-by coffee shop. There are a thousand different ways to initiate a conversation here.

I was on a business trip in Florida and, after a long day of travel, found myself in a hotel elevator with a large, slovenly looking man. As I pushed the button for my floor, he looked me over and asked, "Are you a hooker?" I was mortified and more than a little shaken. I gave him a dirty look and didn't respond to his question. I made sure the man didn't follow me to my room.

Hours later, I found out that there was a quilting conference at the hotel. The participants called themselves "hookers."

This man had a good opening line, but he used it on the wrong person.

Not all of your openers will zing; however, an opener should engage the listener and lead them in to what you have to say. Take these conversation starters and apply them to your speech. I could use the hooker example to give a presentation on quilting or on how to handle harassment when traveling alone. Or a speech on modern infrastructure might include an introduction about why elevators have televisions in them.

Sometimes, a matter-of-fact introduction to a speech will work. State your name and your title, and then tell people what you want to talk about:

"Hello, I'm Cecilia Alcur and I'm the lead scientist at Research, Inc. I'm going to tell you how probiotics will improve your health." If you're having a conversation with the fictitious Dr. Alcur, you might be interested enough to ask, "What are probiotics?" or "Please do tell me how this works." If you're listening to her speech, you would likely want to hear a bit more.

Regional openers are also a popular way to begin a conversation. In Washington, DC, it is common for someone to ask, "What do you do?" In other areas of the country this might seem haughty or irrelevant, but in DC, it's a great way to learn what interests someone and how they are connected. In other communities, the old-timers want to know who your kin is or who was in your high school class. This helps establish relationship ties.

A politician might open a speech with, "It's so nice to be with you here in Midtown today. My pop-pop used to hang out at Doc's soda counter before the building was torn down. Boy, I miss hanging out with him, drinking a chocolate shake while spinning on those swivel stools. Let's talk about how we can build more small businesses in this great town."

Similarly, you might start a speech by sharing something about yourself. A tired father might say, "Thank you for having me here today to speak about electric vehicles. Pardon the pun, but, while I find this topic electrifying, I am admittedly a little sleepy today since my wife and I had our first baby last week. This will also explain the spit-up on my jacket's lapel. That aside, I want to discuss how electric vehicles will create a more sustainable world for us and for the next generation, like my new daughter."

I heard an impromptu speaker use increased voice volume to gain attention at the start of his talk. He bellowed, "Good morning!" in a very friendly manner, and then said, "Isn't it annoying when your mom tries to wake you up this way at six a.m.?" He then discussed his topic, "Early to bed and early to rise makes one healthy, wealthy and wise."

Similar salutations are effective at making sure the audience is paying attention. Speaking after lunch can be one of the more challenging time slots since many people become drowsy after eating and sitting. Sometimes, I offer "good afternoon" to the audience. If they do not respond with the same, I will repeat "good afternoon" until they offer greetings back to me. This can help focus all eyes on you.

Another way to begin a speech is by asking intriguing questions. If you plan to speak on water conservation, you might begin by posing some statistics, like: "Think about how much water you use on a daily basis. Do you keep the water running while you brush your teeth and wash your face? Five gallons of water pour out of your tap every minute. Did you need to clean a shirt and some underwear for today's meeting? Your washing machine used forty gallons of water for that load. I hope you flushed the toilet too, but that means anywhere from 1.6 to seven gallons of water was used with each tug of the handle. Are there simple ways to conserve this precious resource? Yes, and I'm going to tell you how."

Telling a story is another way to captivate your audience from the start. The story might be about you, someone you know, a particular incident, or something you read. Whatever it is, it needs to be relevant to the topic of your speech. For example, someone speaking about nonprofit services might begin, "I was walking down a city street when I came upon a man sitting on a piece of cardboard. He was propped up against the side of some concrete office building. He had a number of worn blankets draped around his shoulders. While his pants were dirty and tattered, his smile was brilliant. He greeted everyone who walked by but did not ask for anything. It was clear that this was his home and that his worldly possessions were gathered in the sack beside him. I responded to his greeting and asked how he was doing. He said he was fine but that he could really use a tube of toothpaste. I was taken with his straightforward request. I asked if he had a favorite brand and then veered off my path to duck into a drugstore to buy him the item. I went back and handed him a bag with the tube of toothpaste. He thanked me, and we both went about our day. It made me think about all the other people who had a need for such basics. It prompted me to start my nonprofit, "Basic Belongings."

Introductions are simply beginnings. They are the prologue to what you want to express in your talk. They should draw in the audience and state the speech topic clearly. How you choose to do so is only limited by your imagination.

Make a Point

You know what you want to discuss, have researched the topic, and have made a general outline of the points to emphasize. Now you need to begin speaking.

If you've written your oration in full, practice speaking one section—or one point—at a time. How does it sound to you? Can you clearly identify the argument or idea you want to express? If you are speaking to a practice audience, ask if they understood your point. You may need to make adjustments.

Listen to the evidence that supports your point. Is it strong enough? For example, if you are using absolute words like "always" or "everyone," then I can tell you that the basis for your argument is weak. Which of the following two statements is more supportive?

A. All airlines should stop distributing peanuts as a snack because some passengers are allergic. Besides, everyone likes the mini pretzels as a substitute.

B. In a survey of 1000 passengers from five leading airlines, when asked which complimentary snack food they prefer, 55 percent said mini pretzels; 25 percent said chocolate chip cookies; and 20 percent said peanuts.

As you read each point aloud, your evidence should be as convincing as B (the correct answer).

As you hear yourself speak, listen for the flow of words and reflect on whether they make sense. You might have a plethora of great supporting evidence, but if you just deliver a data dump of details, the audience won't stick with you. As you speak, you need to take the time to expand on each thought and incorporate transitions from one to the next. Here are two fictitious examples:

C. Running is good exercise for your heart. The national heart society says people who run twice a week have less congestive heart failure than those who do not run at all. An American running club says people who run two miles a day live 4.5 years longer on average. The northwest regional cardiology coalition says 38 percent of patients who run as part of their weekly exercise have lower blood pressure than those who choose to walk or swim.

D. Running is good exercise for your heart. Even though I'm an avid runner, don't take my word for it. National and regional heart- and cardiology-based organizations back up this claim with data and published studies. To name a few, a study by the national heart society shows that people who run twice a week develop less congestive heart failure than those who don't run, and the northwest regional cardiology coalition found that 38 percent of patients who run as part of their weekly exercise have lower blood pressure than those who walk or swim. With these indicators, is it any wonder that the American running club found that people who run two miles a day live on average 4.5 years longer?

With each point, consider whether you need to expand on an opposing viewpoint. When you speak the section aloud, listen for the fullness of your stance. Using example D above, if you are speaking to the local swimming club or if your overall topic is "running is the best sport," you might modify your talk as follows:

E. Running is good exercise for your heart. Even though I'm an avid runner, don't take my word for it. National and regional heart- and cardiology-based organizations back up this claim with data and published studies. To name a few, a study by the national heart society shows that people who run twice a week develop less congestive heart failure than those who don't run, and the northwest regional cardiology coalition found that 38 percent of patients who run as part of their weekly exercise have lower blood pressure than those who walk or swim. Swimming had the second highest rate of patients with lower blood pressure, at 27 percent. With these indicators, is it any wonder that the American running club found that people who run two miles a day live on average 4.5 years longer?

When you say the words aloud, the aim is to sound natural, not robotic. You may be reading a speech, but does it sound like you? Until you speak the words aloud, it can be difficult to hear your own voice and make the necessary adjustments.

You may find it's appropriate to insert a personal anecdote or incorporate more of your own speaking style. On the written page, a sentence might read, "According to NASA, the core of the sun is approximately 27 million degrees Fahrenheit." If you have a folksy speaking style or you want to impress that temperature upon the audience, you might add, "And man is that hot!"

If your written speech is peppered with big vocabulary words that you don't know how to pronounce, you won't know it until you speak the words. It's not necessary to struggle over saying "mischievous" when "wicked" will do. You don't have to impress others in your talk about healthy foods by stumbling over "quinoa" when "whole grains" will usually suffice.

In my neighborhood, there is a common street name that has a distinct pronunciation. If you come to my parts and say it incorrectly, we know you're not from around here. Only if you speak aloud your points will these idiosyncrasies appear so you can adjust for them.

While your intent may not be to memorize your speech, by repeatedly speaking your main points in advance, you may commit portions of it to memory. You may still read your speech from a manuscript, but your delivery will be smoother because you have repeatedly spoken it aloud. You will be less tongue-tied and have more confidence.

If you plan to speak extemporaneously, the same tips apply. To practice expressing each of your points clearly and effectively, assign yourself a topic and speak aloud one argument you wish to make. Listen to how you construct the points you make. Are you incorporating the needed evidence? Does your flow sound natural?

It's not necessary to be perfect in your delivery. You might hesitate to retrieve just the right word to use. In the excitement of speaking, you might forget a piece of evidence or inadvertently reorder the thoughts you planned to express. That's okay. Until you work through the process of speaking out loud, it may startle you when this happens and it might thwart your confidence. After you've dealt with these foibles during practice, you'll find it's much easier to work around them when speaking to a formal audience.

Creating an illustration or using a metaphor to highlight your main points is another way to help you recall what you want to say and draw the audience in to your talk. Let's say your topic is childrearing in the twenty-first century, and you want to describe as one of your points how parents should combat negative environmental influences. You might use the analogy of a mama bear protecting her cubs. Or, when discussing international relations, you might describe a point on consensus-building as "herding cats."

You might also use literary descriptions to bring across a point. For a speech on the US Census, a quote from Shakespeare, "What's in a name? That which we call a rose . . ." might be used to illustrate a point about the census's collection of ethnicity data.

Try using this technique as you speak the words aloud. Are you comfortable using these illustrations? Do they effectively support your point? If so, you might gather several to keep in your back pocket to use in any number of speeches. They may help you make your point.

Another tip is to have common objects act as a prompt for your point. Before you begin practicing, take a look at your surroundings. If you're in a classroom or conference setting, there are common objects that can actually help you recall your points. Take these for example:

Light switch: Reminds you to *switch* to another point.

Light bulb: Stirs you to discuss your idea in depth.

Book: Prompts you to quote a source.

Water bottle: Reminds you that your speech *contains* three points.

Phone: Encourages you to *dial in* your speech to its conclusion.

If you're speaking in a larger venue, there are additional prompts to consider:

Graduation caps: Reminds you of your capstone point.

Tree: Prompts you to think of *growth*.

Flags: Encourages you to flag issues of concern.

Notice your surroundings and incorporate the clues that they radiate. It may help you present your points in a more fluid manner. This is not a skill set that you just stand up and demonstrate. Only by speaking aloud in your practice rounds will you gain the confidence and skill to utilize these tips.

If you're speaking on a subject in which you are an expert—or one with which you are at least very familiar—it may sometimes put you at a disadvantage. You might be "too good" and too smooth in your delivery. If you're speaking before a group of similarly endowed colleagues, it may not present a problem. Yet if you are addressing folks that don't understand the subject matter but wish to learn more, you must speak at their level.

I attended a meeting on metagenomics where national experts presented technical issues related to mock communities, microbial enrichment and extraction methods, and global harmonization. While I have a working understanding of the subject matter, it was dizzying to process some of the wonkier data presented. A brilliant friend with a number of advanced Ivy League degrees was seated in front of me in the auditorium. Half-way through one of the many speeches, she turned around and said something to the effect of, "This conference is giving me a headache."

When you practice aloud, you should be able to hear yourself well enough to know if something might be incomprehensible. A good clue that you're doing it wrong is if you use too many acronyms. The audience may not understand your jargon. Even if they have a basic idea of what you're talking about, you don't want the audience to have to "do the math" in their head in order to comprehend your speech.

Early in my career, I would hear people deliver speeches on "hick-fa." There were many parts of health policy with which I was familiar, but it took a while to equate "hick-fa" with "HCFA," which stands for Health Care Financing Administration. Once I figured it out, the speeches flowed better for me, but why complicate your message? Similarly, when speakers name drop "ACS," are they referencing the American College of Surgeons, the American Cancer Society, or the American Chemical Society? You'll catch these idiosyncrasies within your points as you speak them aloud.

It's the same concern if you use big words. If you're speaking to a room full of general surgeons, it's fine to discuss cholecystectomies, but if you're speaking to a local men's club, it's better to explain a gallbladder removal. If you're presenting before a plumber's union, go ahead and mention the use of pipe flanges, but if the audience is a condominium association, it's better to describe instead how pipes are connected.

Since my father is a physicist, my high school classmates thought I had it made for our notoriously difficult physics class. If I needed a homework assist, all I had to do was ask dad. My father subscribed to the Sheldon Cooper model of teaching. To learn anything, you had to break it down to understand the basics and the history first. Physics was excruciating—not the class, but the lengthy after-class tutorials from my father. Yet, from a public speaking perspective, it's what you need to do with complex topics: break them down and speak them simply and clearly so they are understood.

Once you hear yourself speak, you can modulate your points to your audience. A sales manager might present the latest financial targets to a dozen internal colleagues and whip through accounting terms like EBITA (earnings before interest, taxes, and amortization) or ROI (return on investment) while outlining a national sales plan for the year. The same sales manager, when presenting to outside shareholders, might focus the presentation more on the details of the sales plan, speak more slowly, and use fewer acronyms when discussing the financial projections.

As you practice aloud, keep track of the time. If you're speaking without notes, you may ramble as you explain a point. That's okay at first, but the more you speak it, the more concise your message will become. Aim for brevity.

As you repeat phrases aloud, it's easier to figure out how to trim away the unnecessary parts. When rehearsing, I will often repeat one or two paragraphs over and over again until I think they make sense and flow better. There may be a desire to over-explain a point in writing, but when you speak it aloud, it may sound convoluted. The same goes for reciting statistics. By all means, use supporting evidence, but make it understandable. Reading the financial statement of a Fortune 500 company is not necessary when telling us your main point is that the company crossed a $100 million sales threshold. Brief and simple is best.

Finally, when making your main points, remember this: The audience won't recall every word of your speech. Yes, I realize *you* might. In fact, you may lie awake at night reviewing each word before the big day, or review them endlessly in your mind afterward. The audience, on the other hand, will remember how you made them feel. They should be able to reel off your main points when you are finished, but they will not remember every word you said. They may recall a story you told or repeat a humorous phrase, but that's about it. Keep that in mind as you speak and evaluate your main points. Make them clear, understandable, and memorable.

The End

As you wrap up your talk, think about what message you want to leave with the audience. Here is where you want to remind them of your points, make your final persuasive pitch, leave them with a moral to ponder, or inspire them. It's where you reiterate the purpose of your speech. Yet the words alone are not enough—it's how you say them.

As you rehearse, listen carefully to how you speak the words. Are you delivering them in a monotone? Are you rushing because, frankly, you're glad this speech is almost over?

Are you repeating your main points just because I suggested you do so? If so, you need to make some adjustments.

To oversimplify, think about how a teacher reads a book to a group of kindergarteners. Usually, there's an expressiveness to the teacher's voice and an overemphasis on the ending. You can almost hear a pre-school teacher read, "After making so many friends, the koala bear climbed back up the tree to go to sleep. He couldn't wait until the next sunrise so he could play with them all again."

Likely, the teacher would emphasize certain words, like "so many" and "couldn't wait." The teacher might speak in a lower pitch when saying the words "go to sleep" and in a slower pace when reading the last words, "play with them all again." The expressiveness helps students ponder the meaning of the story. Hopefully, they leave thinking of how to make friends.

I'm not suggesting that you express your public speeches as if you're speaking to a bunch of five-year-old children, but do think about how it takes more than words to bring your purpose home. Adjusting your pitch, pace, and pauses may help.

A State of the Union speech often outlines funding priorities for a presidential administration. A president might start by stating that the union is strong, list those priorities, and then conclude (sound like a familiar speech structure?). After listing twenty-some points, even the most skillful orator might lose the general audience. That's why you'll often hear a closing like "Make no mistake about it: With these priorities, we are and will continue to be the strongest nation! God bless America." Again, you can almost hear the words being spoken. The president will raise his voice during this line and emphasize the words "we are and will continue to be the strongest nation." It is said loudly and proudly. It is a rallying cry and a patriotic affirmation, part of the purpose of the speech.

A speech about art installations in public domains would likely not have as forceful a conclusion. Instead, it may be more beneficial to employ contemplative pauses. Consider these closing words: "Art enriches our community. It allows us to express emotions, recognize rituals, commemorate historical events, and provide entertainment. Public installations allow all to enjoy, discuss, and interpret art. They bring peace, harmony, and color to our world." You can read it as written, but if you pause slightly after each point, "express emotions," "recognize rituals," "commemorate historical events," and "provide entertainment," it allows the listener to conjure up their own vision of these words, making them more impactful and persuasive.

If you just finished giving a highly technical speech on company financials, use your voice to bring home the real message. You might close with a line like, "You just heard all the numbers—$2.4 billion in revenue, $1.2 billion cost of goods sold, $102.4 million in depreciation, gross of $954,679, and a net income of negative $94 million. The bottom line is, with our projections, we are on pace to topple all top three competitors combined." The numbers, likely an important source of support for your main points, are not as needed in the conclusion. Here you might recite those numbers very rapidly, almost as if they didn't matter, and then pause and state clearly, "The bottom line is . . ." You could emphasize the final "to topple all top three competitors" with your voice, and then state "combined" in a louder tone.

If you're unsure how to use emphasis in your own speech, ask someone else to read a passage aloud for you. You might hear what's missing when you listen to someone else.

You want your conclusion to tie up the pieces of your speech.

If you began your speech with a story or an example, you may weave it into the conclusion as well. For example, a speech on immigration law might begin with a tale about the personal experiences of a war refugee. The conclusion of that speech might tell the audience what happened to the individual (maybe that individual was you). In other words, at the end, finish the story that you started in the introduction.

Similar to a story, if your speech is intended to persuade, wrap up with how your recommendations have encouraged positive change. For instance, if you speak extemporaneously on how to promote personal responsibility for the environment, conclude with an example of how your recommendations motivated a group of individuals to improve their behavior.

The same idea works for a speech that begins with a quotation, a saying, or a poem. The introduction opens the page and unveils your purpose; the conclusion knits it all together. Perhaps you begin with a quote from Winston Churchill's speech to the British House of Commons in October 1938: "This is only the beginning of the reckoning." Then you continue with your own contemporary speech on dangers faced by the world's democracies. After outlining your main points, you conclude by saying, "As Sir Winston Churchill foresaw in 1938, democracy too will 'arise again and take our stand for freedom as in the olden time.'"

If you ask questions in your introduction, answer them in your conclusion. You may remind the audience briefly of your supporting points, but close with the message you want to convey. The conclusion is not the time to introduce a new point.

The conclusion is also an opportunity to urge the audience to take action or feel uplifted. A speech on the importance of public speaking might conclude by encouraging the audience to speak up themselves. Or, after a rash of violence, a community leader might conclude public remarks with words to unite and calm a frightened neighborhood.

You can help the audience find the right emotions for processing your talk. You might leave them with a provocative question to ponder. If you are giving a speech discussing the necessity of the Consumer Product Safety Commission, you might close by asking the audience how they would feel if it was their child who suffocated because of a defective product.

You may also use the conclusion to invoke imagery. This is where the speaker will paint a scene with words to bring the speech together. In a speech on which European country serves the best pastries, the conclusion might describe the winning nation's soft and buttery confection filled with a fluffy vanilla cream and topped with an aromatic caramelized cinnamon-sugar.

The conclusion is also a time to clear up anything that might be confusing. Maybe you can tell that your audience is skeptical of your main points. They just aren't buying that a banana diet will help you lose twenty pounds in a month. Yes, they listened as you cited information on vitamins, nutrients, and fat, but no one seemed eager to peel a yellow plantain after the talk. If so, your conclusion might wrap it together by saying that you sense the skepticism, but that you lost thirty-five pounds in under two months on this diet and you've never felt better. Or you can lean in to that skepticism and acknowledge it by saying, "All the points I mentioned about vitamins, nutrients, and fat are true, but the banana diet didn't work for me. I wouldn't suggest it for you either."

The audience needs to know that you have finished your speech. You will often hear people end with "thank you." It's not really clear what they are thankful for—maybe that they don't have to talk anymore? It's a rote reaction for many orators to say simply "thank you," but it's not the strongest closer. At least inform the audience of *why* you are thanking them: "Thank you for listening to me this afternoon. I hope I have encouraged you to put on your sneakers and go for a run today," Or: "Thank you for considering this action. I would be glad to answer your questions."

Instead of the "thank you," use transitions to signal the end of your talk. Your last sentence might begin with "In conclusion," or "The last thing I want to say is," or "Remember this." The pitch, pace, and pause in your voice will also let the audience know the ending is here.

Sometimes speakers will overindulge the audience. You'll hear, "Thank you for being an amazing audience," or, "I loved being here with such a fantastic group today." Generally, the audience is just sitting there listening to you. Unless there was a 6.7 magnitude earthquake during your talk and no one left or ducked under their seat, why is that considered so amazeballs? Don't overdo it.

The end is not the place for unintended drama either. Don't give the ultimate mic drop, stop speaking, and leave the stage immediately. The audience will think you're dissing them and they won't know why. Instead, stop speaking, wait a few moments (the audience may applaud), back away, and confidently leave the stage. You might even nod toward the moderator or host to indicate that you are turning the platform back over to them.

The end of a speech should not mirror the closing credits of a blockbuster movie where everyone is recognized, from the actors to the producers to the assistants who fetched coffee on the film set. It's okay to thank people, but don't make these your parting words. You don't want your lasting impression to be the people you thank instead of the actual substance of your speech.

Remember, the conclusion is where you can shine and bring across the purpose of your talk in a meaningful, engaging way.

Chapter Seven

Be Nice

Be Courteous

Let's talk about manners. Even in public speaking, there are etiquette rules. They are not written in stone, per se, but they make a difference in how you are perceived.

Years ago, a famous comedian was performing at a local theater. On the stage was a stool and a small wooden table. The disheveled comedian was in a grouchy mood. For all I know, this was his usual state of mind, but he was noticeably irritated at something. He had with him a fistful of notes. He began by reading his notes to the audience, explaining that he just wrote these jokes and wasn't sure if they would work. He said we, the audience, would be his testing ground to see if he would keep any of this material for future performances. He read aloud one vulgar page after another. Everything, from his lack of performance effort to his disregard for the ticket-paying audience, was disrespectful. Some people walked out, including me. As a speaker, it's simply not how you want to be perceived.

In truth, when it comes to public speaking, many people are unfamiliar with how to act. Yes, there are differences—be they regional, ethnic, or other factors—that may influence a speaker's behavior. Yet there are common courtesies that we should all strive to abide. Being courteous, or nice, is something that should be second nature. Below are a few tips to set you on the proper course.

Introduce yourself. You know who you are. Maybe 90 percent of the people in the audience know you too, but chances are someone hasn't met you. Maybe they see your name on the agenda but haven't confirmed you are really you. Tell them. It's as simple and courteous as saying, "Hi, my name is Jonathan Pierce" (or whatever your name is).

I'm generally asked once a month to provide a presentation to about sixty people in a local auditorium. I like to think I know everyone in the room, or that they know me, but it's not always the case. My name is written in the agenda, but unless I tell them, someone may be scratching their head wondering why I'm there. Inevitably someone will approach me after the talk to say, "Oh, I've heard about you, and now I can finally put a name to a face."

Be nice. That's right, being darn right nice goes a long way. You will help create a more pleasant atmosphere and do your part to elevate humankind. If that's not enough of a reason, being nice will reflect well on you. When judging forensics competitions, I am struck by the contestants who say "please" and "thank you" and are courteous of their fellow speakers' time. It may not change how I judge their speaking skills, but it certainly enhances their presence and professionalism.

Respect others. As a speaker, show regard for other people. Easy ways to show respect include showing up on time for your presentation and being prepared. It's rather crummy to begin by arriving fifteen minutes late and then adjusting and testing the microphone to your liking, all while the audience watches and fumes over your rudeness. This behavior shows a lack of consideration for the time and feelings of others. Arrive promptly—or, better yet, get there early to work out all the kinks.

Other ways to demonstrate respect are to listen to other speakers and wait your turn. You should want to hear what others say. Watch, listen, and learn from their presentations. Don't fiddle with your phone or gossip with other attendees; give each speaker your undivided attention.

Your speech should show respect too. When others contribute to your work, say so. A lead manager or team captain should acknowledge others in the room who added to a presentation. It may be as simple as, "My talk today on how we can improve leadership skills within our company would not be possible without the input received from Corrine Bailey and Graham Ravi."

Of the numerous authors whose book talks I've attended over time, David Sedaris is one who certainly made me smile. Tears of laughter streamed down my face while reading his book, *Me Talk Pretty One Day*. He was just as witty in person, but what stayed with me was his generosity. Instead of plugging his own books specifically, he advised the audience to read one by a new author, Aleksandar Hemon. So much time has passed since that talk (even the bookstore has closed), but what remains is Mr. Sedaris's humor, liberality, and outstanding recommendation.

Remember never to belittle or embarrass the audience. You may know more about a subject than others, but don't flaunt it. If someone asks a question, acknowledge the importance of the question. You might say, "Thank you for that question," or, "I appreciate you giving me the chance to clarify," or, "That's a great observation; let me discuss it." It will make the audience member feel good that you showed the respect to consider their issue.

Stand tall. There will be situations when you should stand, if you're able. If the audience is on its feet for you when you enter the room, you, too, should be standing. If a moderator is seated when introducing you, you may be seated. When the moderator finishes the introduction, you may rise to stand, if that's the conference protocol. Standing, if you're able, is generally seen as a sign of respect.

Try not to stand in front of someone else. It is considered rude to have your back to another person. Some room arrangements will make this point difficult to heed. If you're a graduation speaker, chances are there will be rows of professors seated behind you. There's not much you can do about it. But if you're in a meeting room and find yourself blocking someone, take a few steps to the side to avoid this faux pas.

Be honest. It is essential to be truthful in the words you speak. This is for the sake of your own integrity and reputation as well as for the audience, who deserves to hear accurate information. While you may not intend to lie about the facts and figures you present, it is dishonest to exaggerate or distort details in your speech.

If you are giving a speech on the greatest chess champions of all time, it would be dishonest to say that only one grandmaster never lost a match when, in fact, that grandmaster played half as many matches as his nearest competitor. Instead, make it clear that the grandmaster, while still a worthy titlist, played far fewer games.

Calm down. It's not uncommon to get a little stressed before a talk. Take on healthy activities that lower your stress levels. A warm bath or an invigorating run the night before your speech may help. Have a light dinner so as not to upset your stomach, and have a fortifying breakfast to give you energy. Right before your speech, steal a few minutes to take a brisk walk around the block or in the hallways to clear your mind. Of course, keep drinking water to stay hydrated.

Don't cuss. Don't use profanity during a formal presentation. One curse word may be funny if used in the proper context, but frequently spewing trash usually makes the speaker sound trashy. It may also make the audience uncomfortable.

Have fun. Whether you are addressing agricultural commodity markets in Asia or enlightening the room on tomato varietals, enjoy what you do. The audience can tell if you don't want to be there. Whether you love public speaking already or you are still working up the nerve, have a good time!

Civilly Disobedient

Etiquette is the code of conduct that polite society follows. Let's face it: Sometimes somebody will get under your skin—yes, even during a public speech.

One of the best examples of speaking gone wild is the British Parliament, where lively debate is de rigueur. Yet even in these public exchanges, there are customs to follow, such as standing to address the body and wearing formal business attire. In fact, the House of Commons issued a booklet in November 2018 on "Rules of behaviour and courtesies in the House of Commons," which outlines the rules for civil discourse.

There are ways to disagree civilly while minding our manners.

Witty repartee is one way to bring across a biting criticism in a cordial way. The late Texas governor Ann Richards was well known for her folksy colloquialisms that hammered on policy or political opponents. When giving the keynote address to the Democratic National Convention in 1988, Governor Richards had this to say about debts her opponents had amassed: "It's kind of like that brother-in-law who drives a flashy new car, but he's always borrowing money from you to make the payments."

In your speech, you may wish to express your disregard for a person, policy, or idea. A masterly, funny put-down may work, but it should never be cruel or demeaning to an individual or group of people. Speaking ill of someone, especially about features they cannot control, should be off-limits. Remember, when you speak poorly of others, more often than not it will reflect poorly on you—rather than your intended subject.

Try to be clever. If you're delivering a speech on bioscience policy and you disagree with an approach, you might say, "The only culture it possesses is bacteria." Maybe you want to express strongly to an audience of medical professionals how a particular health policy issue is a pain in the butt. Use the word "coccydynia" to get your point across.

If you want to explain how an opposing view is nonsensical, you might say, "This policy will work when pigs fly," or "What a bunch of malarkey." If you speak of a policy that seems deceptive, you might say, "It's like doing the hokeypokey, but you can't turn yourself around." Make sure you back up these assertions with facts in your speech.

Go ahead, be wicked. If you have something biting and pithy to say and it fits your talk appropriately, say it. But remember this: When the years go by and your great grandchildren want to write a history report about you, will your speech make them proud?

Hahaha

"A priest, a rabbi, and a minister walk into a bar . . ." Many of us have heard these time-worn jokes in speeches. Sometimes they are funny, sometimes they aren't. Sometimes they are really, really offensive. Friends of mine who abhor giving speeches feel pressure to be funny and deliver a zinger or two. They needn't worry. Jokes are not mandatory!

In fact, unless you are particularly adept at humor, you're better off not adding jokes. You may think you're funnier than you are. Frankly, unless the joke is specifically relevant to your speech and is not offensive, and you have the talent to deliver the punchline well, it may be best to lay off the humor altogether.

Even personal anecdotes can fall flat. A retiring association executive spoke before an annual gathering of his organization's membership. In his farewell address, he thought it would be funny to tattle on business colleagues who engaged with him in wild escapades thirty years prior. His oversharing left the audience squirming and unamused at the inappropriateness of his behavior.

It is okay to make people laugh. I was speaking at a conference where the host was having a difficult time getting the technology to cooperate. He eventually called for a ten-minute break. After the break, when everyone filed back into the room, the microphone and computer system were still not cooperating. Eventually, with the help of some aides, the host appeared finally to have gotten the equipment working, so the host introduced me and I hustled up to the microphone. I began my speech but only mouthed the words. The audience, and especially the host, looked mortified, thinking the technology was still down. After a few seconds, I spoke up and audibly said, "Nah, I'm just kidding you." The audience giggled and seemed to settle in to my presentation, and we put the technical difficulties behind us.

You may be charming and amusing while speaking. You might laugh at your own comments or raise an eyebrow when a point is questionable. Most of us, however, should just forget about the jokes.

Give Proper Credit

It must be said that if you quote evidence in your talk, be sure to cite the source of the information. Not only is it proper to give due credit, it also heightens your own credibility to have another source support your argument.

When you're speaking, it is usually not necessary to provide an entire citation, but you do need to give credit to someone else's idea. In a speech, you might say, "President Abraham Lincoln reminded us, 'Four score and seven years ago our fathers brought forth on this continent a new nation, conceived in Liberty, and dedicated to the proposition that all men are created equal.'"[ix] It is not necessary to add where, when, and why the president made this statement, unless it is particularly relevant to your point.

Never try to pass someone else's work off as your own. If you presented an oratory on equality and presented as your own words, "I ask you to remember our fathers brought forth on this continent a new nation, conceived in liberty and dedicated to the proposition that all men are created equal," you would be guilty of plagiarizing President Lincoln. You would look foolish to boot.

The same rule applies to facts and figures. If you want to cite trade statistics, note that they came from the US Department of Commerce or a similar source. Unless you're a trade expert who generates and analyzes such data, no one will believe you came up with these stats on your own. Besides, the Commerce Department holds more sway than you do. Let them back you up.

If presenting a prose reading, always state the title of the selection and its author. It's the same for poetry, stories, and dramatic interpretations: State aloud the source of the work. Even if you only read segments of a piece, it's not your original work. If you recite the first and fifth paragraphs of a work and you edit it into a reading, it's still not your original work. Give credit, always.

Chapter Eight

The Impact of Forensics

Forensics is an impactful sport. That's right—a sport. It requires mental agility, just like tennis or basketball. It's competitive, just like football (but with less bruising, one hopes). Social interaction, skill, and hand-eye-mouth coordination are all in play. There is no hand-to-hand combat, like in boxing, but some debate rounds can be intense. I don't expect the Olympics to accept forensics into its lineup of sporting competitions, but there's likely a debate to be had here!

That said, the list of positive attributes forensics fosters is long: self-confidence, poise, critical thinking, research capabilities, composure, communication, friendship, stature, intelligence, collaboration, and teamwork, to name a few. Public speaking programs in college, high school, middle school, and even elementary school should be established and fortified for the benefit of all students.

I am a strong proponent of forensics programs, which are generally considered extra-curricular activities. Yet public speaking as a skill should be incorporated into a variety of learning settings. In second grade, Mrs. Harrison had me speak in front of the class about holidays. In fourth grade, I ran a presidential campaign against my best friend's candidate. In my sixth-grade class, we were paired up and instructed to create a commercial and present it to the rest of the students. These were all public speaking opportunities. These types of activities should be available for all students. Public speaking builds life skills.

This chapter features several people who participated in scholastic forensics programs. You may find it amusing, but not all of them enjoy public speaking! Yet many of them attribute their success in life to forensics. The takeaway is how pivotal forensics can be in a person's life. Whether you are standing up to speak as a student or as a tenured professional, the lessons may be the same.

Richard Osbaldiston

It's hard to believe that Richard Osbaldiston once considered himself a passive learner who didn't understand how to apply himself. Despite believing he lacked a certain agency, he earned bachelors and masters degrees in chemical engineering from Georgia Tech and the University of South Carolina, a masters in environmental studies from Yale, and a masters and doctorate in social psychology from the University of Missouri. Dr. Osbaldiston is now professor and chair of the department of psychology at Eastern Kentucky University.

When I was in tenth grade, my friend Jake stopped me in the hallway to say, "Hey Richard, we're going to start a four-man debate team. Do you want to be the fourth person?" I said, "Sure, that would be great." At first, debate was just a social outlet for me: people to be with and something to do. But then there was this energy to it.

I would be shocked if anybody could be involved with debate, actively engaged with it, without it becoming a positive force in their lives. You learn, when you come up with a concluding argument, how to show evidence to support that conclusion. You learn that not all evidence is equal and that there can be evidence on both sides. You can argue for the quality or the strength of the evidence. That's an incredible intellectual leap to make. I think there are probably a lot of adults who never successfully make that leap.

Everything I learned in high school was through the debate team. The whole process of how to think, how to create an argument, how to express yourself, how to stand up in front of people and risk being wrong, I learned through debate. These are essential life skills. I don't know how I would've learned those things in the traditional education system. I certainly didn't learn much in social studies or Spanish or any other class.

Reflecting back on being fifteen, sixteen, seventeen years old, the debate team really was the singular most powerful force in my life at that time. It is responsible for my development as a young man turning into an adult. The experience was formative. The debate team helped create this identity for me. I don't even recognize it anymore because it is so much of who I am. If you ask my ten closest friends, they would say I am a very analytical, very structured thinker. It came from being immersed in the debate team for those years.

As a professor of psychology, the spiel I give to students is that psychology is a science. Everything we know in the psychological field has to be documented through some sort of experiment or research process. You gather data, analyze that data, and then form a conclusion based on what you see. That's exactly what debate is to me. The topic changes, but the intellectual skill is the same. I use that skill literally every day, practically every moment in my job, because we're scientists.

I don't think I would have naturally gravitated toward public speaking. If you subtract the debate team out of my formative years, I probably would have favored a career where I was more of a mouse, a "seen but not heard" kind of person. But after you deliver a debate a couple hundred times, all of a sudden, you're thinking, "Yeah, I can get up in front of a few people and speak." Once you get that skill, that confidence, you never really give it up. Today, I deliver at least three lectures a day to students.

Public speaking is a skill that works like shooting basketballs. If you want to learn how to shoot free throws, the only thing you can do is get a ball and a basket and shoot. Of the first ten free throws, you're probably not going to hit many. The only way to develop your public speaking skills is to gather an audience and stand in front of them. You have to be prepared for some of your shots to miss the basket.

Christa Arnold

The epitome of cool in school, Christa Arnold was a sensation whether beating on a drum set or striking the marimba. She led the marching band as its drum major and competed fiercely on the tennis court. Yet it's her involvement on the forensics team in high school and college that led to her ultimate career choice: a professor of communication studies at the University of North Florida.

While in school, Dr. Arnold competed in prose, poetry, impromptu, and informative speaking. She competed on the national collegiate level in duo interpretation and after-dinner speaking. Her mother, Peggy, a forensics coach with an infectious personality, motivated her to get involved.

She was very much my muse. She could talk pretty much anybody into anything. My brother was a football player and a bass player. He's a really cool guy. She talked him into going to one of these competitions and doing a duet interpretation with me.

During the duo I forgot my line that was the trigger for my brother to speak. I just kind of stared at him because I couldn't think of my line. As a prompt, he said to my character, "So Nancy, what do you think?" He kept changing the line, three or four different ways. "Nancy, what are you thinking?" I finally recalled my line, but we got tickled by it. We were trying not to break character, but after the performance he said "Nancy, you're not a very bright bulb." We joked about how dumb and dim-witted Nancy was. I just could not think of that line to save my life.

Knowing how to ad-lib and how to keep going under pressure, being able to compete with your brother, having your mother coach you, and then meeting all these new people when you go on these competitions— it's not just an activity, it's an experience. To this day, it has helped me overcome any kind of discomfort of speaking in public, which I continue to do now through seminars, workshops, lectures, and class and conference presentations.

Looking back, I really enjoyed the duo presentation I gave at the collegiate national competition. The piece was one of those quirky little nothing stories that turned into a really interesting duo. It was about two ice cubes in this drink that meet and fall in love. It's this little love story which, in the time it takes to give a duo presentation (five to seven minutes), goes through the whole evolution of these ice cubes meeting and melting.

It's one of those stories that, at first blush, you would've thought was the stupidest story you'd ever read. Forensics took the story and made it really come to life. Between the way it was voiced and the very slight bouncing movement we added to appear like we were floating, it really expressed the feeling of being an ice cube in the water. It touched all these people in the audience. We made some writer's little story about two ice cubes, a story that had been buried in a library, completely come to life.

Forensics is a great academic exercise. It is fun. You meet great people. It is a wonderful activity to put on your college résumé. It's a remarkable skill builder. It just kept opening doors for me.

Leslie Haynsworth

As co-author of the book Amelia Earhart's Daughters: The Wild and Glorious Story of American Women Aviators from World War II to the Dawn of the Space Age, *Leslie Haynsworth uncovered how female aviators had the right skills at the wrong time. Leslie herself has many skills. A doctorate in English led to an assistant professorship at Columbia College, and then to a career in professional writing. Today she is the Director of Communications and Marketing at Heathwood Hall Episcopal School. Speech and debate in high school may have played a role in her success.*

I was not planning to get involved in forensics. I didn't go to the middle school that fed into my high school, so as a freshman, I was the new kid trying to make friends. The people I got to know and hang out with were mostly involved in forensics and they were so enthusiastic about it. Eventually, I decided to try it. Honestly, my big interest was riding horses, which I did every Saturday and Sunday. It conflicted with going to weekend debate tournaments.

So, sophomore year, I tried a couple of forensics events. I started out performing dramatic interpretations, at which I don't think I was very good. Then I moved on to original oratory and extemporaneous speaking. In my senior year, I did two-person debate, mostly as a novice, which was sort of weird for a senior, but it was my first year with it. I think I realized that debate was actually the activity I liked best. I won the state championship in novice Lincoln-Douglas debate my senior year, along with my debate partner Jessica Deysach. I actually quit riding horses.

I definitely learned to think on my feet. I have memories of doing extemporaneous speaking and having to prepare with all these note cards. I needed to know where I could get my hands on information in really short time. It took preparation. It was a fantastic learning experience, as was Lincoln-Douglas debate and regular debate. It was really good preparation for college, where so much of the writing that I was asked to do was oriented toward making an argument.

I work in marketing now, but earlier in my career I was a professor. Just standing up in front of people and being okay with talking to a bunch of people—that training really helped.

Everyone who was involved in forensics seems to have had their horizons expanded in some way. Some kids from the suburbs would call us the "inner city kids" and appear sort of scared to come into town to hang out with us. We thought it was funny since we didn't think we were living in a rough, urban area.

Having a circle that extended beyond my high school was a great experience. I valued getting to hear what other students were thinking just by sitting through their speeches. In a usual high school classroom, so much of your work is individually generated so that only the teacher sees it.

I learned a lot by listening to peers. Most of all, don't try to be who you think your audience wants you to be. Own who you are and be as comfortable with that as you can be when you're speaking. You're going to be most compelling when you're authentically yourself. People are usually going to respond to you even if you seem different from them or different from what they want.

Glenn Lightsey

An aerospace engineer who worked for NASA's Goddard Space Flight Center, Glenn Lightsey is a popular professor at Georgia Tech. A recipient of the American Society for Engineering Education's John Leland Atwood Award for outstanding aerospace engineering education, he directs the Center for Space Technology and Research at the university. Dr. Lightsey was also selected by the National Science Foundation to collaborate with NASA and a team of universities on a new space mission to expand our understanding of the sun. Before his career ignited, Glenn shined as a different type of star.

I actually started out in drama. I liked acting and did a very small amount of television and stage acting in middle school and high school. I was in a couple of episodic shows, bit roles, as well as high school plays and very local productions. As a progression from acting, I moved into forensics. I really enjoyed the camaraderie of working with a team. It was exciting to get in front of people and speak and be evaluated on my performance. I liked that aspect of it. I think it helped provide a forum for practicing and improving my skills.

In high school forensics, I most remember the pace of it. In going to tournaments, it was pretty intense for a couple of days. Every round of the competition presented a different case. You have to be mentally alert and flexible to adapt your reasoning to whatever situation you're presented with. It was interesting how you argue both sides and debate it. There was no right or wrong, just the question of whether you are in favor of an issue or opposed to it. It taught me a lot about ethics and that there can be many different views on a complex topic. The logic, ethics, and morals of debate gave me a more rounded perspective that stayed with me through my life.

I work on spacecraft technology to advance the state of the art. I really enjoy it. I realize when you think of aerospace engineering, you don't really think of forensics. They don't come to mind right away as programs that might be related. But it's important to recognize that engineering in itself is a team-oriented profession. You work together on large projects and you communicate with people. That communication is extremely important because you are often addressing technical topics where precision is paramount. Strong communication skills can often be the difference between success and failure on a project.

The ability to communicate effectively, both verbally and in written form, is very important in engineering. A lot of people miss this point. They think, "Oh it's just equations and math." Yet those communication skills have stayed with me, and it's really important for my ability to do my job. I do research with my students, and I teach classes several times a week for a hundred students. That's basically forensics, right? I'm describing something complex to an audience. The confidence it takes to do that, the feeling that you can step in front of people and say something important that conveys knowledge, is a skill I was able to develop during forensics. It really became part of my career.

If you had asked me in high school whether I would be using forensics in aerospace engineering, I don't know if I would have understood or appreciated it, but I certainly do now.

Jessica Tew

Jessica Tew was always involved in a wide range of activities. In high school, she announced musical selections at band concerts, competed in forensics, and scooped a mean cone of Baskin-Robbins ice cream while raising money for school activities. As an undergraduate at Harvard, she produced an ice-skating show that raised funds for the Dana Farber Cancer Institute, rode crew as the lightweight team captain, worked at the library, and traveled to Wales on a Rotary Scholarship. She earned her medical degree, finished a fellowship in pediatric endocrinology, and practiced as a pediatrician. After her children were born, Dr. Tew decided to focus her energies on them. In her free time, she's a national seminar coordinator for the American Needlepoint Guild.

One of the things I've done as an adult, that I always wish I did earlier in life, is take piano lessons. I've been taking lessons for twelve years now. No one has deprived the world of any great piano virtuoso. It's funny, but I have such nervousness of playing in front of anyone else. In fact, I can't even practice if I know somebody is listening to me. Yet I don't feel that way about speaking in front of people. It's very similar, I tell myself. You're reading the music and the notes, which is like reading a page while speaking. If I missed a piano note, it would freeze me completely. I would have to go back and fix it. Yet if I'm speaking and miss a sentence, I can make it work and have the speech make sense as I go along. I think forensics played a huge role.

Forensics helped me to converse. When you work on extemporaneous speaking, people lob questions at you. So in interviews, you can stand on your feet, you can answer the questions, and you can speak confidently. It teaches you how to be assertive without being grating or condescending.

I'm from South Carolina, and we are sometimes viewed as backwards and maybe not that intelligent. I think being well-spoken, with the ability to minimize my accent, was an asset. Forensics made me able to communicate clearly so that people maybe think I'm more intelligent than I actually am or that I am more in charge than I normally am. People will listen to me.

These lessons connected with me when I finished my pediatric residency and was starting a pediatric endocrine fellowship. The clinical department asked me to conduct research on sheep with polycystic ovarian syndrome. There was a possibility that I could get my own grant from the National Institutes of Health to support it, but I had to make a presentation on the topic.

The department flew me up to Ann Arbor, Michigan, where I was to give a thirty-minute talk on a topic that, quite honestly, I had just researched. I had the confidence that I could do it if I had the information. Having had those experiences of standing up in front of people, getting to practice those skills through the years, and the coaching and the friends that took me under their wing, encouraged me. I received the grant.

When I was growing up, I didn't know about the various careers available to me. I figured I'm good in science. I like science, I like people, I like kids, and I can get into medical school. This seemed like a good thing to do—good security. By the time I became chief resident, I had to speak frequently, introduce speakers, and all that kind of stuff. I can get up in front of a crowd, and I don't care how big it is. I can read something that's given to me cold and be fine.

Forensics attracted a wide range of kids. Some of them were popular athletes and some had no other activities of interest. It brought together a mixture of the artistic and the intellectual. From the dramatic interpretation people to the debate team, despite all the different backgrounds, you were all on the same team. You rooted for each other and you had the same goals. Success didn't always mean that you won the prize. If you stood up and did well, or improved on your last speech, that was success. Public speaking gives you confidence to feel successful even if you aren't number one.

In high school forensics, my big thing was dramatic interpretation. Heart-wrenching pieces like *Sophie's Choice* were ideal for me since I could make myself cry on cue. The forensics team put on a play to raise money for tournaments. I was cast as an old lady and I still put on that voice every once in a while just to be silly. Looking back, I think forensics would have been a good launching pad for other opportunities. I don't think I had the skills, or the looks, or whatever it would take to become a big movie star or television actor, but had

I known about it, I may have chosen to do voiceover audio work. If I had known more, I might have found a different career.

Laurie Jarrett Rogers

Laurie Jarrett Rogers is a grant writer for nonprofit organizations in Richmond, Virginia. She focuses her efforts on matters that serve children, youth, and families. She says the fulfilling work of identifying funding for these programs consumes her world. She also teaches courses in fundraising at the University of Virginia, Virginia Commonwealth University and the J. Sargeant Reynolds Community College Workforce Development Program. Laurie is not afraid to speak up. In fact, her husband lovingly jokes that she's "sometimes wrong, but never in doubt."

I'm a grant writer. Writing a grant to a foundation is like telling them a story. You only have 2500 characters or 150 words to tell your story. So how do you do that? You do it the way you've been trained. You have to pick the most salient points of your argument. So, whether I'm on a high school debate stage or sitting in my home office writing to the Mellon Foundation, I'm making a point. I'm making an argument for this funder's support of my program and my client's program.

Debate taught me how to make that point and how to make it succinctly.

Rather than turning in a ten-page proposal, like I used to be able to do twenty years ago, now you get a paragraph to answer the world's biggest question. So what will you say? What message will you convey? Every time you open a new application, you face a whole new set of questions. How will you prepare for that? It's like a debate prep exercise. For me, that was a skill I got in high school: how to prepare.

You remember the dark days of no computers and card catalogues? You pulled the cards out of the drawer and then you went and found the book. It just seems so antiquated, but that's how you had to prepare. You had to check out articles at the library. You had to think about the time it was going to take you. It's about time management.

It's about how you structure your day. How do you organize your thoughts? If you're researching something, how do you bake in the time to your schedule to go to the library and use a card catalogue to check out the book? Those were some really important skills. The fancy term for it is "executive processing skills." I absolutely believe that debate was one of the activities that helped me with that.

Back in the late 1970s, early 1980s, we didn't have words like that. The word *executive* and the word *functioning* were in our vocabulary, but not together as a term of art. Now it's one of the things they focus on in high schools: He or she does or does not have strong executive functioning skills. It helps explain why students are getting their work done, or why not. I never called it that, way back when. I certainly didn't think about it as any kind of time management skill, but that's the lasting effect of it. That is how it plays out for me.

Whether I'm talking to a full auditorium or to a workshop seminar with fifteen people, I rarely get butterflies about standing up. I can get in front of any microphone. I can stand up in a class. I can stand up in a group of people. I have no problem with that. There had to be a seed planted in that high school debate experience.

Edward Pittman

I always thought Edward Pittman would become a judge, given his studious and fair-minded nature. My premonition was boosted by Edward's convincing portrayal of a jurist in his high school's production of WhoDunDidIt, *a play written by Peggy Arnold and Christa Arnold. It turns out he pursued an equally weighty career. Edward is Portfolio Manager of New Jersey's Public Pension Fund, whose assets hover around $80 billion.*

My father was in the military, and we moved around a couple of times. I grew up in Virginia Beach. We moved to Naples, Italy, before I started seventh grade. I moved to South Carolina to my grandparents' house midyear in ninth grade. I didn't know many people. At the end of ninth grade, I received a letter from Mr. Goldie, the debate coach, asking me if I was interested in debate. It never occurred to me to participate, but I decided to try a summer debate preparation where we spent lots of hours in the University of South Carolina library.

I remember studying the *Congressional Record* from the 1980s and reading carefully all the research on seatbelt usage and airbag laws. The debate topic was consumer products, and our case supported a mandatory seatbelt usage clause, which at the time wasn't very common. Other people had cases on requiring airbags, which are now universally installed. Then there was one year where the topic focused on arms sales to other countries. I learned a lot about US-China policy, the Middle East, and sales to Saudi Arabia.

Learning about current events and public policy was one of the benefits of participating in debate. Now, when I'm designing school financing systems in New Jersey, being able to analyze public policy issues has been beneficial. We have about 500-plus school districts in our state. State funding is largely used to help lower income school districts equalize funding to create a fairer system. There is never enough money to do what people want to do. There are trade-offs. Debate gave me not just public speaking experience, but also the policy analytics experience. It is a useful skill set for me even today.

I can't say that I'm involved with public speaking at work, but debate and forensics were very helpful in pushing me to be a better communicator. It helped me academically. It was part of my motivation for getting my own kids interested in debate, or something called "public forum," at their high school. Digging intensely into a topic is a great discipline.

Shira Miller

A frantic call that my college professor received led to my own amateur career as a forensics coach. It was the speech and debate coach of Dreher High School calling. He was preparing to take his students to a tournament, but the competition was in jeopardy because there were not enough judges. My coach couldn't do it, so he asked if I'd like to fill in.

I soon found myself in a car with the coach, Richard Goldie, and a handful of high school students. One of those students was Shira Miller. Shira was earnest and bubbly. It was her first tournament and she wanted to do well, so I gave her some pointers. On the ride home, she decided I was going to be her big sister. Mr. Goldie seemed to have a similar idea. While dropping me off, he asked if I'd consider coaching the forensics team at Dreher while he focused on the debate team. From that moment, the Dreher High School forensics team became my family, just like Shira had decided.

Today, Shira makes all kinds of decisions as the Chief Communications Officer for National DCP, a $2 billion supply *chain management company serving the franchisees of Dunkin'. Earlier, she started an eponymous public relations firm representing clients such as Spanx, California Pizza Kitchen, and the American Turf Council. She writes frequently about wellness and self-improvement, and says that public speaking changed her life.*

I can't say it more dramatically. All of the goodness, all of the reaching for more, and showing myself that I had potential and could accomplish so much—it all came from public speaking.

It meant a lot to have my parents be proud of me. I had wonderful parents, but I grew up in a very small world. In high school, I was monogram-sweatered, freckle-faced Shira. I was the kid growing up who tried tap, jazz, ballet, sewing, gymnastics, soccer, you name it. None of it connected. Yet with speaking, it was like, Kaboom—I was home. I discovered I was good at it. It opened up so many doors. Speaking exposed me to what was possible. It put me in contact with a whole different caliber of people who were going to really good colleges, who were doing interesting things, and who were thinking bigger thoughts in life.

Without learning public speaking, I would not have aimed as high. I would not have realized things that are possible. I would have almost settled without knowing it. Of course, it isn't settling if you don't know it's settling. Yet I think I would have had a much smaller life, and would never have pictured the life I have now. Public speaking showed me so much of what was possible.

Speaking became a pillar of strength for me, no matter what I was dealing with over the decades. I even discussed this in my 2019 TEDxBoggyCreek talk, "5 Ways to Let Go of a Dream."

Public speaking taught me analytical thinking: how to set up my argument, how to organize my thinking, how to be persuasive, and how to entertain a crowd. Those are life skills that help you excel no matter what you do. Traditional education doesn't teach you that, but public speaking did and it helps me to this day. It's that kind of thinking that helped me get ahead in the beginning of my corporate career thirty years ago.

I would say wherever you are in your life, whether you are young or midpoint in your career, whether you want to gain more confidence or to shine, public speaking can help enrich you as a person. It will build your skills and confidence.

Greg Howell

Greg Howell is a leader. Not because he was senior class president in high school (he was), or because he directs research administration at a leading national cancer nonprofit (he does), or because he has worked with major universities in obtaining grant funding for research (he has). Greg leads because he is mindful of the value of others.

Ms. Christine Webb was so important to our high school, Dreher, and its reputation as a great school for academics. She was the principal from about 1975 to 1986, which was a very critical time as Dreher was still struggling with desegregation. I remember talking with her about it. Education and excellence were so important to her. She recognized that an opportunity like a debate team was something a top school should have. She would have done everything she could to make it happen. She was a strong leader and she listened. She's an inspiration still.

I've always been interested in public speaking, at least trying to learn to get better at it. I thought that high school forensics would help. At an initial orientation at the coach's house, I saw a good group of people. There were impressive upperclassmen involved. There was the coach, Mr. Goldie, who was a really interesting and knowledgeable person. He had a clear passion for debate, and that added to the appeal of becoming involved.

I remember going to tournaments in Gatlinburg, Tennessee, and at Davidson College. I thought we did pretty well, and Mr. Goldie seemed pleased with my performance. A lot of times I would sit up front in the car and chat with him on these long tournament trips. It provided interesting perspectives.

The camaraderie of forensics should be emphasized. I made good, good friends in class, and I forged even deeper friendships with members of the debate team. It was another bonus of being involved.

All these experiences definitely have an impact on you. It gave me an interest in policy and in issues, and the ability to understand some of the nuances. Issues are not black and white. Debate helped me some with public speaking, but it forced you to talk quickly and get as many arguments out as you could in the time frame provided. Extemporaneous speaking provided more of a focus on speaking to persuade a normal audience.

Overall, forensics helps you to think critically and be concerned about issues. We were always looking at the details, the statistics. Then we had to go behind the statistics to check the credibility of the source. If we didn't, our opponent could. Forming arguments that were truthful and doing our own research were some of the skills I learned and developed more in depth.

Deborah Carter McCoy

Deborah Carter McCoy teases that she was brought up by the Socratic method of parenting. Whenever she expressed an opinion as a child, her father would quiz her and ask what evidence she had to back it up. These interrogations served her well. When she entered high school, she participated in a forensics summer camp and was intrigued by the research aspect of public speaking. Research plays a major role in her career as director of strategic communications for a growing nonprofit organization that focuses on equitable environmental solutions.

I love data dives. I love looking at research studies. I'm in a professional association where I help facilitate learning programs around transportation research. As a student of knowledge, I love organizing facts and data. Back in high school debate, that really appealed to me. I knew how to use the library and I knew how to answer questions because of my father. But debate, and the intensity of that research, is where it sparked.

I remember being so impressed when I got to hear other people speak. In high school, we were all reasonably intelligent, but it just felt very glamorous and exciting on top of it. Traveling to tournaments as a group was such a good bonding experience. I have nothing but fond memories of debate.

Forensics helped me develop a level of comfort with public speaking. I still don't like it. I'm still very self-conscious. I'm still very aware of fumbling with language, but I can do it and I'm not terrible at it. The skills that I learned there have helped me help other people develop skills and confidence speaking whether at a conference or in front of a camera. As a media liaison and spokeswoman, a lot of my job over the years has been to coach people in that way. I listen for things like: Does the speech flow? Does it make sense? Is it interesting? Are people going to learn something? I also want to know if people are going to be curious about the topic and if they're going to ask questions.

It's okay to stumble. It's probably better to stumble over your words than to say "um" every three minutes, or every minute, or, hell, every ten seconds. I did learn a lot back then that I use today.

I like a southern accent. I moved up to Minnesota and they were like, "Where are you from, mama?" making fun of me. It's taken a while to really embrace that it's okay to have an accent. In fact, it's interesting to have an accent. What I learned in speech and debate, in forensics, was to show up as yourself. Underneath the performance, underneath the debate, or underneath the dramatic interpretation is the person. So developing a comfort level with who you are, how you speak, how you sound is really important. It helps develop a core sense of self-confidence that translates across really anything—from picking up a phone and making a cold call to giving a presentation.

It sounds a little melodramatic, but forensics was probably life-changing for some of us. It ended up being a really incredible outlet. I remember hanging out, and we would talk about dumb stuff that teenagers talk about, but then we would talk about really profound stuff too. You want to be around people who are insatiably curious about the world and you want to explore it with them. I think that opportunity was really incredible.

Nicholas G. Meriwether

Nicholas G. Meriwether recounted how he was asked by the director of the South Caroliniana Library, a major scholarly repository of Southern history and culture, to write an article on the library's founder, his grandfather. He agreed to the task, though he shied away from the family connection in the essay, focusing instead on his grandfather's work as the founder of the prestigious institute.

While this may be genteel modesty, the truth is the connection is irrelevant. Nick's scholarly work on nineteenth-century Southern intellectual history stands on its own accord. The publication of the article led to Nick joining the South Caroliniana Library as its oral historian. While there, Nick added to his Princeton and Cambridge education by earning a library science degree with a focus in archives and oral history. His larger work on American Bohemianism and the American counterculture led to his appointment as Grateful Dead Archivist at the University of California, Santa Cruz. Today he serves as Director of Museum Planning and Development at the Haight Street Art Center in San Francisco, where he curates exhibitions, and is a nationally-recognized scholar, writer, and speaker. While his high school debate experience may have sown some of that talent, he says he has a real dislike of public speaking.

It's funny, I also have a tremendous fear of heights. Yet when I was in graduate school, I went skydiving—twice. The only thing it did was actually reaffirm that fear. In fact, the second time was worse than the first. So I think of public speaking as the same kind of thing. I don't think you ever really get over that fear, but what you can do is learn to deal with it. You can be a good public speaker even if it's not something that you're particularly oriented toward. Debate was a way of accomplishing that for me.

The larger lesson is that you're always going to be confronted by fears and weaknesses throughout your life. How you choose to deal with that is a big part of what will define you. Acknowledging that you have those fears and then dealing with them anyway is an enormously important experience.

My father, who was a college professor, said that, in his opinion, debate was one of the most important things in my high school career. It did a lot to sharpen my analytical and writing skills. It taught me how to research. All of that was nothing but positive, nothing but good.

The downside was the fact that it's adversarial and competitive. I came to that realization when I was a high school senior. Debate helped me get into college, but it was something I knew I didn't want to do once I got there. It was all-consuming in high school. It was great training, but I think many debaters also came to see the real downside of that adrenaline-fueled competitiveness. I was much more interested in seeing what could be accomplished through cooperation and collaboration, and less about the kind of gladiatorial pitting of positions and ideas that high school debate fostered.

A significant chunk of my scholarly life has been spent writing and publishing on the Beats and the hippies and the counterculture after World War II. It's a sprawling movement. There's a very real critique of citizenship that animates many segments of the counterculture. It frayed the civic conversation that we have today, contributing to the fractious and divided political spectrum that teaches the limits and pitfalls of that kind of clash. For example, a debate case might win a national competition because it was better argued and better researched, yet, ultimately, it wasn't a viable blueprint for national policy. In high school debate, I wish I could have seen more of a discussion of intellectual character and the ethics of certain positions, not just their utility or sheer argumentative power.

In the hands of a skilled debater, almost any argument could win. That certainly doesn't undercut the skills of doing good research or thinking your way through things. If you think you want to be a scholar, then debate is an absolutely superb building block. There is no better training for learning how to structure your argument and express it in a lean and concise way.

My scholarship today is still in many ways informed by the genesis of the skills that debate taught me in high school.

James Assey

Before serving in his current role as executive vice president for NCTA – The Internet and Television Association, where he represents cable television and broadband providers, James Assey spent many years on Capitol Hill as a legislative aide and as counsel to a US Senate subcommittee. Prior to embarking on that career in Washington, DC, James was awarded the Annenberg Fellowship, which made him an American ambassador to Eton College, the largest boarding school for boys in the United Kingdom. While he was there, his public speaking skills put him in high renown.

I got to live in a fairytale for a year. I taught at a famous British boarding school, Eton College—very kind of upper crust. All the boys there wore long, black morning coats and these very stiff, starched white collars with ties and everything. They had so many rules to follow at Eton. I was out of college and probably closer in age to these boys than I was to most of the other teachers, who had been there for twenty or thirty years.

One of the requirements of this position was to give an address to all of the classes and the teachers. I didn't know what to pick for my topic. I decided (and maybe

I was feeling a little bit rebellious because of all those rules) to give my speech on the value of coeducation—to an all-boys school. It went over really well with the boys. I got a lot of raised eyebrows from the teachers. I remember making a well-organized, sometimes tongue-in-cheek argument for the benefit of co-education. When I closed and put my hand on the lectern, about three hundred boys rose to their feet with wildly enthusiastic applause. I don't think it had anything really to do with my speech. I think it was more because I was sticking it to the other professors in the room. It was a very memorable experience.

The ability to stand up in front of an audience and tease an argument all the way through was something I honed and worked on in the process of forensics. I do a lot of public speaking. I'm now an advocate. I'm a lobbyist for an industry. In this situation, you're not always engaged in a debate where you have to unpack opponents' arguments point by point. It's not a competition to make three points for every one of theirs. Yet forensics definitely sharpens your analytical skills. It made me comfortable speaking. It made me very practiced on how to build an argument, how to use my voice, and the inflection needed to make a point or to emphasize something.

In high school, I did novice four-man, which consists of two teams with two debaters each, and extemporaneous speaking. When you go to your first tournament, you don't really know what to expect. Obviously, you've practiced, but when you first see somebody launch into a spread, or they're talking so fast and you're frantically trying to write down notes, there's an immediate, kind of overwhelming, sensory aspect to it. You're thinking, "What's going on here?" Then it's almost like you're deciphering Aramaic or something. You start to figure out how to follow what they're saying, how to take notes, how to listen to their argument, and how to think quickly on your feet to be able to respond. There's a little bit of an adrenaline rush in being able to participate in that kind of an environment.

There was a social aspect to it too. We got to travel all up and down the Eastern Seaboard. As freshmen in high school, we didn't do too many things that had us actively working with seniors and juniors. So it was pretty heady stuff when you were just starting out and you got to spend so much time together with them researching, practicing, or traveling to tournaments. These were some of the closest friendships that I made. Eighty percent of the people I still keep in touch with from high school I can trace back to the time we spent on speech and debate.

You also got exposure. We felt like we were the cocks of the walk in South Carolina, but then these tournaments introduced us to some of the other programs. And holy moly! It was just really impressive to see Montgomery Bell or Bronx Science or Detroit Catholic or some of these other national forensics programs and realize there's a whole world of people out there. That was cool too.

I have a second grader and she's getting to that point where she's becoming quite argumentative. Sometimes I look at her and hope she does debate. As much fun as I got out of it, I can see already that she's got it in her too. Whether or not she wants to tap into it and participate, I don't know. It is something that certainly has guided me in life. I know that I had a positive experience with it. I hope she's able to try it out one day too.

Marshall Elson

In high school, our forensics club would sometimes adver-tise its meetings over the school's public address system in the morning. Our club wanted more students to join and prayed that at least one soul would walk into our after-school enclave to see what it was all about. While the roar of a crowd was never to be, one day, seemingly out of nowhere, a boy appeared. He was painfully shy and shuffled his feet slowly across the class-room carpet. He wouldn't—or couldn't—make eye contact. His gaze was intently focused on his shoes. As club president, I gin-gerly asked if he was interested in joining the forensics club. He nodded affirmatively. For years, I had no idea how he mustered the courage to enter the room. Marshall Elson is perhaps the greatest success story of them all.

After coaxing from our coach, Mrs. Fillmore, and his fellow students, Marshall decided to try delivering an original oratory, a prepared speech of his choosing. He practiced relentlessly and made it to the district competition. More importantly, by the end of the year, Marshall would walk the halls with his head held high. I heard that he eventually ran for, and won, a spot in the leadership of the local Future Farmers of America (FFA). Decades later, I found Marshall, now a biological science laboratory tech-nician at the US Department of Agriculture (USDA), and asked what gave him the courage to walk into that room.

Initially, I was encouraged to do it by my parents. They knew that I was pretty shy and they thought I'd get less shy by participating in speaking contests. I soon realized that if I practiced the same speech over and over again, I was able to memorize it. Once it was memorized, I could deliver it in front of a few people. Often during forensics competitions, there weren't many people in the room. I could handle the small numbers.

My first speech in tenth grade was about wind power. In my senior year I delivered a speech I wrote about vanishing farmland. By then I was speaking at contests for the forensics team and the FFA. I progressed through various levels of forensics competition and eventually placed second in the state. The FFA was a different story because the audiences grew much larger. The FFA state competition was held in the auditorium at Burruss Hall at Virginia Tech. Burruss Hall is a major historic venue on the college campus, and its auditorium held over three thousand seats. I kind of choked on that one. I got so nervous.

After high school, I received my bachelors degree in landscape horticulture. The program required a public speaking class, but it was different than the earlier forensics competitions. We would have to give a different speech each week, so I didn't have the time to memorize them. It wasn't as comfortable to me as giving one speech multiple times.

Forensics gave me confidence in knowing that if I had prepared my speech, then I could get up there in front of people. Yet I was too shy to do well in interviews. I wanted to be a landscape designer, so I went through four years of college and did well in the landscape courses. I got my first job after graduation, but I wasn't good at the selling part of it. I wasn't very successful at that, so I went back to school with the idea of becoming an extension agent. I went through a couple of years of training and started doing research. I liked doing research. So then I went to Michigan State to get another degree, this time in horticulture with a specialization in vegetable crops. I thought, "Well, now I'm going to be a college professor." I applied for about two hundred jobs, got half a dozen interviews, and didn't get any of those positions.

I didn't get the job I was wanting in part because I was too shy to do well in the interviews. Now, as a scientist with the USDA, I conduct experiments and analyze data. I still have social anxiety, but when I give presentations to groups, I do the same thing I learned years ago in forensics. I write out my speech, I memorize it, and then I can get up in front of a small group of twenty or thirty people and talk.

Forensics gave me the confidence that allowed me to do new things. At one point in high school, the members of our team were asked to go on stage individually in front of a full auditorium of students and give a short speech. I was nervous doing it, but I had practiced the thing repeatedly, so I got out there and did it. By the end, a whole bunch of people in the auditorium started chanting my name: "Marshall! Marshall!" They wanted me to do another one. It was a fantastic feeling.

You Be You

Public speaking can be tough. It's like a first date. You may be nervous asking the person for a date, or you may be apprehensive about accepting a date. Eventually, you get up the nerve to do it and you introduce yourselves to one another. Then you have points to share that may be informative, entertaining, or persuasive. As the date winds down, there is a conclusion that might lead you to accept another one. Let's assume you were nice, appropriately dressed, and poised.

In public speaking, like when you're on a date, think about what you want to share with others. No matter the speaking format you select, what is it that you want to say? Are you irked by a city policy for enrolling kids in camp? Do you want to advocate for a greater tree canopy in your neighborhood? Do you collect antique cameras and want to share your knowledge? Are you proud of your rebuilt car and looking to inform others about the mechanics? Are you an expert in the microbiome who wants other scientists to hear your perspective? There are people waiting to hear from you. Yes, YOU!

You don't have to be a national speech champion or a TED conference speaker, although kudos to you if you are! You don't have to become the go-to conference keynoter. You just have to take the first step to speak up. I promise your voice is worth hearing.

NOTES

[i] "World AIDS Day: Prince Harry reveals fear of public speaking." BBC News. December 1, 2014. https://www.bbc.com/news/av/uk-30272563 (accessed June 6, 2021).

[ii] Goss, Betty. "Public Speaking." Thomas Jefferson Foundation, Inc. January 9, 2001. https://www.monticello.org/site/research-and-collections/public-speaking (accessed June 30, 2022).

[iii] Chapman University. 2021. "The Chapman University Survey of American Fears Wave 7." Orange, CA: Earl Babbie Research Center [producer]. https://www.chapman.edu/wilkinson/research-centers/babbie-center/_files/Babbie%20center%20fear2021/the-complete-percentage-list-of-fears-2020-highest-to-lowest.pdf (accessed June 30, 2022).

[iv] Begala, Paul. "Comparing Obama's Health Care Speech to Clinton's." Interviewed by Melissa Block. All Things Considered. September 9, 2009. https://www.npr.org/templates/story/story.php?storyId=112685196 (accessed July 17, 2022).

[v] Burra, Nicolas, Hervais-Adelman, Alexis, Kerzel, Dirk, Tamietto, Marco, de Gelder, Beatrice, Pegna, Alan J. "Amygdala Activation for Eye Contact Despite Complete Cortical Blindness." *Journal of Neuroscience*, 33, no. 25, (2013). doi: 10.1523/JNEUROSCI.3994-12.2013 (accessed June 6, 2021).

[vi] "Television: Larry Hagman: Vita Celebratio Est." *Time*. August 11, 1980.

[vii] "Taking Care of Your Voice." National Institute on Deafness and Other Communication Disorders. Last updated April 15, 2021. https://www.nidcd.nih.gov/health/taking-care-your-voice (accessed June 6, 2021).

[viii] Institute of Medicine. 1999. Marijuana and Medicine: Assessing the Science Base. Washington, DC: The National Academies Press. https:doi.org/10.17226/6376 (accessed June 30, 2022).

[ix] Lincoln, Abraham. "Gettysburg Address." Speech, Gettysburg, PA, November 19, 1863. https://www.loc.gov/pictures/resource/cph.3g12220/ (accessed July 17, 2022).

CPSIA information can be obtained
at www.ICGtesting.com
Printed in the USA
BVHW031304260922
647986BV00017B/490